ACHIEVEMENT
ENGLISH @YEAR 11
CLOSE READING OF
UNFAMILIAR TEXT

NELSON
A Cengage Company

Australia • Brazil • Japan • Korea • Mexico • Singapore • Spain • United Kingdom • United States

Achievement English @ Year 11: A Close Reading of Unfamiliar Text
1st Edition
Jenny Thomas
Diane White

Cover design: Book Design Ltd and Cheryl Smith, Macarn Design Ltd
Text designer: Book Design Ltd and Cheryl Smith, Macarn Design Ltd
Production controller: Siew Han Ong
Reprint: Natalie Orr

Any URLs contained in this publication were checked for currency during the production process. Note, however, that the publisher cannot vouch for the ongoing currency of URLs.

Acknowledgements
Illustrations courtesy of Brenda Marshall.

Our grateful thanks to all past and present colleagues who have so generously shard their expertise, creativity and resources. English departments thrive on you collegiality.

The authors and publisher wish to thank the following people and organisations for permission to use the resources in this textbook. Every effort has been made to trace and acknowledge all copyright owners of material used in this book. In most cases this was successful and copyright is acknowledged as requested. However, if any infringement has occurred the publishers tender their apologies and invite the copyright holders to contact them.

Page 6, Under the Mountain courtesy of Maurice Gee; page 7, A Windy Day courtesy of Andrew Young; pages 8-9, advertisements courtesy of Kiwibank; page 15, The Modern Girl's Guide to ... Swimming Togs courtesy of NZ Women's Weekly and Sarah-Kate Lynch; page 17, Fewer Children go to school on foot - study, 2008, courtesy of Giles Brown, Fairfax New Zealand Limited; page 18, A mountain of stupidity 2008, courtesy of Fairfax New Zealand Limited; page 20, Love and Other excuses courtesy of Jane Westaway; page 26, Greasies to go ... courtesy of The New Zealand Herald; page 29, Routeburn courtesy of Mike White and North & South/ACP Media Ltd; page 34, So Gay courtesy of Steve Braunias and Sunday Star Times, image courtesy of Getty Images; page 37, Extract from The God of Small Things by Arundhati Roy published by HarperCollins Publishers, London, 1997. Reprinted by permission of HarperCollins Publishers Ltd. © ; page 41, Wintery Gloom, courtesy of David Montgomery (Tommy Gorden); page 43, Preludes courtesy of T S Eliot and Faber and Faber Ltdl page 45, Pet Shop courtesy of Louis MacNeice and David Hingham Associates; page 47, Grief on the Whanganui River courtesy of Anne McDonnell; page 49, Being Sixteen courtesy of Michael Khan; page 51, Kite courtesy of Anne French; page 53-54, The Lady of Shalott courtesy of Alfred Lord Tennyson; page 57, painting by William Holden Hunt courtesy of Manchester Art Gallery Picture Library; page 60, advertisement courtesy of Land Transport Authority; page 63, advertisement courtesy of The Auckland Museum; page 65, advertisement courtesy of GlaxoSmithKline page 68, advertisement courtesy of DairyNZ; page 72, Why Don't Your Talk To Me? courtesy of Alistair Campbell; page 73, Compulsion courtesy of Tania Kelly Roxborogh; page 75, Mana Wahine courtesy of Terri Hudson; page 72, Thistles courtesy of Faber and Faber; page 81, Cook's Sites. Revisiting History courtesy of Otago University Press; page 83, The Mess We Made at Port Chalmers, courtesy of Cilla McQueen and Otago University Press; page 84, extract courtesy of Forest and Bird.

For product information and technology assistance,
in Australia call **1300 790 853**;
in New Zealand call **0800 449 725**

For permission to use material from this text or product, please email
aust.permissions@cengage.com

National Library of New Zealand Cataloguing-in-Publication Data
Thomas, Jenny, 1972-
Achievement English @ Year 11 : close reading of unfamiliar text / Jenny Thomas and Diane White.
ISBN 978-017026-490-7
1. English language—Composition and exercises.
2. Comprehension—Problems, exercises, etc.
I. White, Diane. II. Title.
808.042076—dc 23

Cengage Learning Australia
Level 7, 80 Dorcas Street
South Melbourne, Victoria Australia 3205

Cengage Learning New Zealand
Unit 4B Rosedale Office Park
331 Rosedale Road, Albany, North Shore 0632, NZ

For learning solutions, visit **cengage.com.au**

Printed in China by 1010 Printing International Limited
9 10 11 12 13 14 25 24 23 22 21

Contents

LANGUAGE LIST

When you see this icon refer to pages 87 and 88 for a detailed list of the terminology used in relation to that text type.

1. Year 11.

You've made it to the first Level!

YEAR 11 IS A REALLY IMPORTANT YEAR.

You have graduated from the junior school to the senior school.

Year 11 is probably the year when you will tackle external assessment for the first time. You've been working towards this throughout Year 9 and Year 10 and you will have absorbed many of the essential skills you need to succeed at **NCEA Level 1**.

Think about what your work was like at the beginning of Year 9. You'll see that you've already learnt a lot!

Achievement English @ Year 11: Close reading of unfamiliar text is designed as a workbook for you personally to use to support your study of English this year. It will:

- help you hone your skills
- give you lots of useful practice
- give you plenty of good advice about how to achieve in English this year.

All of the examples and exercises have been chosen with you in mind and with reference to the kinds of assessments you will find in both external and internal Standards.

We are confident that you are ready to begin,

so let's get going ...

ISBN 9780170264907

Check it!

⊶ What does all this really mean?

Close Read	Reading for meaning
Comprehension	Understand
Unfamiliar Text	Enlarge
Precise	Interpret
Analyse	

A key skill in the study of English is to understand and analyse text, and as you already know, a text might be a novel, a short story, a magazine article, a poem, a poster, a still from a film, a business card etc. The skill of close reading applies to *everything* that you read, view or hear. And it is going to be increasingly important to be able to show your understanding of significant aspects of visual, oral and written text as you progress through senior school. This is not a skill that can be taught in isolation.

While it is true that your assessments will separate the close reading of unfamiliar written text (AS 1.3) and visual and oral text (AS 1.11), if you think about it you are actually using these skills in virtually all aspects of your English course, and in actual fact much of the assessment in your other subjects too!

This part of the book is designed to support the close reading instruction and practice in your classroom with your teacher. It is not just a way to answer particular assessments.

In *Achievement English @ Year 11: Close reading of unfamiliar text* we have chosen to present the methods for close reading in one section. So don't be surprised when you find a section on visual text in this section … remember when you work with Achievement English you are learning skills, not just practising assessment.

ISBN 9780170264907

Before we go forward, let's go back

Let's make sure that you have some of the essential terminology that you will need this year. We will be focusing on Close Reading, but you will use your knowledge of the terminology for English study in all aspects of your course this year.

We are going to begin by giving you three texts to look at, so that you can check where you are up to in your knowledge of terminology.

Things to do with prose ...

This year you will be expected to analyse different types of prose: fiction, non-fiction, extracts from novels, short stories, magazines, newspapers etc.

This extract, from Maurice Gee's novel *Under the Mountain,* is describing a warm, protective light around three-year-old twins lost in the bush. People are searching for them.

Read it carefully and then complete the task on the next page.

Indefinite article

A light like a flame was moving in the trees, so bright it made them hide their eyes. It floated high above the ground, turning like a mist through the trunks.
'What is it?' They ran over the clearing, but as they ran it vanished, and they stood bewildered in the weak glow of their torches. In that same instant, deep back in the bush, the light came down beside Rachel and Theo Matheson. It covered them like a blanket, flowed round and under them, soft and honey-coloured, drew down and dulled itself. Warmth flowed into the limbs of the sleeping children. They smiled and murmured. All night they slept as though in their beds at home. They dreamed happy dreams. The light lay still and warm over them, murmuring like a hive of bees.
Greyness came through the black night of the bush. Trucks and cars roared into the Matheson farm. Policemen, farmers, gathered for a second day of the search. Dogs barked. A helicopter chattered down the valley from the town.

ISBN 9780170264907

We want to use this short passage for 'the naming of parts'. When you have read the passage, use the list below and find as many of the elements as you can. Highlight and annotate each term.

We have done the first one for you.

Parts of Speech
- ✓ Indefinite article
- ○ Definite article
- ○ Verb
- ○ Preposition
- ○ Pronoun
- ○ Possessive adjective
- ○ Common noun
- ○ Proper noun
- ○ Adjective
- ○ Conjunction

Syntax
- ○ Simple sentence
- ○ Compound sentence
- ○ Compound-complex sentence

Figures of Speech
- ○ Simile
- ○ Alliteration
- ○ Repetition
- ○ Personification
- ○ Onomatopoeia

LANGUAGE LIST

Things to do with poetry ...

You will also be expected to read and understand poems. Sometimes students believe that this will be difficult. Remember, poems are simply the best words in the best order.

Read this poem carefully and then complete the task on the next page.

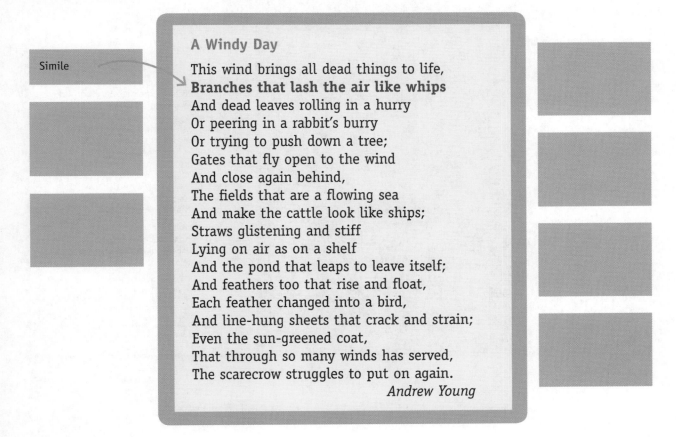

Simile

A Windy Day

This wind brings all dead things to life,
Branches that lash the air like whips
And dead leaves rolling in a hurry
Or peering in a rabbit's burry
Or trying to push down a tree;
Gates that fly open to the wind
And close again behind,
The fields that are a flowing sea
And make the cattle look like ships;
Straws glistening and stiff
Lying on air as on a shelf
And the pond that leaps to leave itself;
And feathers too that rise and float,
Each feather changed into a bird,
And line-hung sheets that crack and strain;
Even the sun-greened coat,
That through so many winds has served,
The scarecrow struggles to put on again.

Andrew Young

Find, highlight and annotate as many examples of the following as you can:

Parts of Speech
- ✓ Simile
- ○ Metaphor
- ○ Personification
- ○ Alliteration
- ○ Onomatopoeia
- ○ Repeated structure
- ○ Rhyme

LANGUAGE LIST

Bonus Point:
Can you remember why an author would use a semicolon?

When you have looked carefully at the poem and you have seen how many figures of speech the poet has included, you will appreciate that he has illustrated beautifully what happens on a windy day. You might draw a picture from these words.

Things to do with visuals ...

The third type of text you may be asked to analyse is called visual text. This may be an advertisement, a poster, a book cover etc.

Visuals have an additional set of techniques which you need to be aware of – techniques to do with layout and colour, balance, contrast, symbols etc.

Read this visual text carefully and then complete the task on the next page.

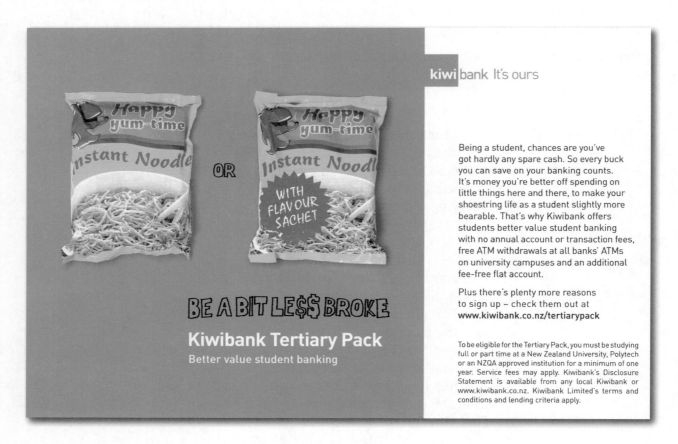

ISBN 9780170264907

Using both these advertisements, find, highlight and annotate these techniques:

Same product. Different audiences. How can you tell?

_____

_____

_____

_____

⌐○ How did you go?

We have just asked you to find 45 features of language. Look back over your work. How many did you find?

- If you found 40 or more, you're ready to move on.
- If you found 30-39, use the language list at the back of this book to remind yourself of what you have forgotten.
- If you found fewer than 30, then it might be a good idea to go back to *How to … Achieve in Year 10 English* for a refresher course!

Close Reading – learning to read and understand Unfamiliar Text

You will have been taught how to 'close read' texts every year that you have studied English. In the earlier books of this series (*How to ...* and *Building On ...*) we taught you to analyse text by thinking of the types of questions asked.

1 On the surface

One of the skills that close reading tests is your ability to understand what is happening in the text. Therefore the first type of question you are likely to meet is the basic literal question where the answer is clearly written in the text.

These questions are likely to be based around *facts*. Things such as:
- Who?
- What?
- When?
- Where?
- Why?
- How?

In other words you will be looking for factual information.

2 Technical

You are going to hear the word 'style' quite often when you study English. Style means the way something has been written. To help you understand the writer's craft, you will begin by looking at his or her techniques. This will include things like vocabulary (the words selected by the writer) and structure (the way the sentences are ordered). You will be asked to identify the basic language features.

To answer a technical question successfully, you will need to have some idea about the intended audience, be able to recognise the language used and the way the text has been put together.

3 Search and think

These are implied questions. You will have to 'read between the lines' of the text to answer questions in this section. It is likely you will need to use your own knowledge and thinking, as well as information from the text, to answer these questions.

For many of you these will be the trickiest of all questions because they demand that you think carefully about what is being said and then think about what that means. You may believe this is difficult, but in fact you do it every day. You look at people's body language, tone of voice, the words they choose to use and you make a judgement about how you will respond. Search and think questions ask you to do the same thing. Read the passage and make a judgement about what is going on that is not written about. Read between the lines of the text to answer these questions.

SO TO RECAP ...

- You know the terminology
- You know the types of questions asked
- You know what is required to answer them.

ISBN 9780170264907

HOWEVER ...

At this stage it is likely that you have been taught to look for information, to find techniques and perhaps to comment on the way they create a specific effect. To make progress in your understanding and analysis of text, you need to see how the text has been created as a complete piece, in a planned and deliberate way.

To help you learn to do this we need to introduce the concept of *Style*

You need to see how a piece has been crafted intentionally: in a certain style, with a certain purpose, for a certain audience.

Style

We are sure you will know the word style in connection with fashion. In the world of clothing, style can be formal (school uniform), flamboyant (rapper), grunge (rock band), sporty (athletic), girlie (pink and frilly) etc.

When it comes to the written word, style is *the way the author writes*, rather than what the author writes about.

For example, if four people were at a car accident, and were all asked to write down what happened, all four would probably have a different way of telling the same facts.

A policeman would probably give just the facts, in a very serious, straightforward style.

> 'The Ford Escort was travelling at approximately seventy kilometres an hour along Princes Street.'

A reporter for a newspaper like the *New Zealand Herald* might give a much more sensational and vivid account.

> 'Black rubber stripes along a city street mark the site of a major crash.'

The man whose car had been hit might write in a very angry and emotional style.

> 'A lunatic almost wrecked my Beamer. The idiot charged down the street stupidly ignoring the speed limit. He should be locked up and the keys thrown away.'

The driver might be more defensive.

> 'I was driving along, not very fast, when a huge dog leapt out from a driveway. I couldn't do anything, really. It wasn't my fault.'

TYPES OF STYLES YOU MIGHT COME ACROSS THIS YEAR INCLUDE:

Persuasive   HUMOROUS   *Dramatic*

Emotional   Colloquial   Formal

Be careful ... sometimes a piece of writing might use more than one style.

Think of it as directors creating different types (genres) of films for different audiences: the chick flick, thriller, animation, drama, adventure, political, documentary, wester, sci-fi, art-house etc. Each type is aimed at a different part of the cinema-going audience.

ISBN 9780170264907

⊢O So ... how do we find the style?

The following diagram draws together all of the threads you will use to identify style. It will provide you with a useful reference chart whenever you look at a piece of unfamiliar text.

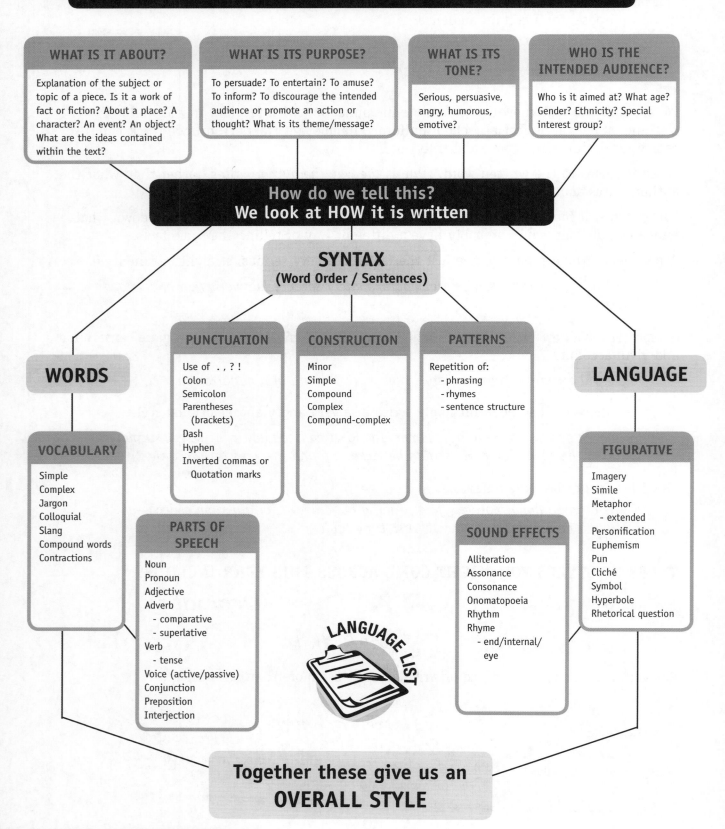

HOW DO WE APPROACH AN UNFAMILIAR TEXT?

WHAT IS IT ABOUT?
Explanation of the subject or topic of a piece. Is it a work of fact or fiction? About a place? A character? An event? An object? What are the ideas contained within the text?

WHAT IS ITS PURPOSE?
To persuade? To entertain? To amuse? To inform? To discourage the intended audience or promote an action or thought? What is its theme/message?

WHAT IS ITS TONE?
Serious, persuasive, angry, humorous, emotive?

WHO IS THE INTENDED AUDIENCE?
Who is it aimed at? What age? Gender? Ethnicity? Special interest group?

How do we tell this?
We look at HOW it is written

SYNTAX
(Word Order / Sentences)

PUNCTUATION
Use of . , ? !
Colon
Semicolon
Parentheses
  (brackets)
Dash
Hyphen
Inverted commas or
  Quotation marks

CONSTRUCTION
Minor
Simple
Compound
Complex
Compound-complex

PATTERNS
Repetition of:
- phrasing
- rhymes
- sentence structure

WORDS

LANGUAGE

VOCABULARY
Simple
Complex
Jargon
Colloquial
Slang
Compound words
Contractions

PARTS OF SPEECH
Noun
Pronoun
Adjective
Adverb
  - comparative
  - superlative
Verb
  - tense
Voice (active/passive)
Conjunction
Preposition
Interjection

SOUND EFFECTS
Alliteration
Assonance
Consonance
Onomatopoeia
Rhythm
Rhyme
  - end/internal/
    eye

FIGURATIVE
Imagery
Simile
Metaphor
  - extended
Personification
Euphemism
Pun
Cliché
Symbol
Hyperbole
Rhetorical question

LANGUAGE LIST

Together these give us an OVERALL STYLE

ISBN 9780170264907

Before we go any further ...

Fill in the gaps.

1. The beat of a poem is called _____.

2. When a non-living thing is given living characteristics it is called _____.

3. A comparison between two things using 'like' or 'as' is a _____.

4. _____ is a specialised language used by people who work together.

5. An _____ _____ is used at the end of a sentence to show strong feeling.

6. You find extra information inside _____.

7. The section of the reading/viewing public at which a text is aimed is called the _____ _____.

8. A _____ is a word that joins sentences.

9. Highly colloquial expressions unsuitable in general conversation are _____.

10. A question designed to suggest rather than demand an answer is called a _____ _____.

11. A _____ sentence does not contain a verb.

12. A phrase used to express a request, order or command is an _____.

13. _____ language is relaxed and informal language used in common conversation.

14. _____ is the deliberate repetition of consonant sounds at the beginning of words.

15. A _____ plays on different meanings of the same word.

16. A writer who wishes to involve the reader will frequently use _____.

17. A _____ is added to the end of a word to alter its meaning.

18. _____ shows the writer's attitude to the topic.

19. _____ is where words and/or phrases are repeated for emphasis or for special effect.

20. _____ tell us how, when or where an action takes place.

Why do professional writers choose certain techniques?

Many close reading questions ask you to not only identify language features but explain why an author has chosen to use that technique. Complete the following grid to assess your knowledge. Go back to *How to ... Achieve in Year 10 English* if you need a reminder.

Technique	Definition	Why used
Simile	A phrase that compares two things using 'like' or 'as'.	
Personification	When a non-living thing is given living characteristics.	
Adverb	Tells us how, when or where an action takes place.	
Minor sentence	A sentence without a completed verb.	
Onomatopoeia	When the sound of the word imitates or suggests the meaning or noise of the action.	
Repetition	Where words or phrases are repeated.	
Pun	An expression that plays on different meanings of the same word.	
Rhetorical question	A question that does not require an answer.	
Assonance	The deliberate repetition of the same vowel sound followed by a different consonant sound.	
Alliteration	The repetition of consonant sounds, usually at the beginning of words.	
Pronoun	A pronoun may be used instead of a noun.	
Colloquial language	Relaxed and informal language that is used in common conversation.	
Metaphor	A phrase in which one thing is identified with another.	
Adjective	A describing word.	

ISBN 9780170264907

Don't panic! Let's show you what we mean

Here is a column from the *New Zealand Woman's Weekly* that has a distinctive style. Read it carefully and answer the questions that follow.

The **modern girl's guide** to...

Swimming togs

FBI ILLUSTRATOR: HELEN CASEY

● At the risk of sounding like a wet blanket, I wish the nicer weather would go away.

It's just I'm lying awake, night after night, worried sick about global warming, the Greenhouse effect and having to buy new togs.

There's something horribly wrong with a world in which the time you need to buy something which covers less of you than anything else coincides with the time when most of you should be kept covered up.

As it is, the first foray – usually about now – into your local tog emporium often ends in severe trauma, resulting from a pale, pudgy woman who looks a bit like you, only sadder, staring out of a mirror. It makes you realise how good you are at hiding stuff.

Of course, it doesn't help that the changing room lights play tricks with your cellulite and those sensible knickers, left on in the interests of hygiene, can hardly be said to add to your allure – like you need more lumps!

As for the helpful assistant who opens the door to see how you are getting on – well, she deserves to be in therapy for the rest of her life. Doesn't she know there are two occasions when a girl must be left in complete and utter isolation? (The other involves chocolate.)

Once, I had a bikini. I think I was seven. I remember it vividly, because the pants were made of towelling and had a porous lining, which meant large amounts of sand became trapped between the layers and gave a pronounced sag.

Now, I have that sag all on my own.

At some stage in my teens, there was a two-piece which involved bikini pants and a short halter-neck dress which covered several regions. This was quite popular – but it disintegrated after about 14 years.

More recently it's become a full-time job traipsing the stores, looking for vertical stripes and rouching in the right places.

This year, though, I got smart.

We're talking mail order. Why risk exposing bits of yourself – which should have been waxed off months ago – in a semi-public place when you can do so in the comfort of your own home, with the curtains closed and the lights turned off?

Having a selection of togs arrive in your mailbox takes the trauma right out of it. You have to be careful not to put the trauma right back in, though.

It helps to have a full-length mirror – poorly lit, of course. At our new flat in Wellington, we only have a bathroom mirror which, for the purposes of modelling my new swimsuit selection, I plonked on top of the laundry basket. This showed me only my thigh and stomach region.

When I came to, I tried putting the mirror on the dresser but this only showed me from the neck up. How could I tell if the floral centre-panel was doing its job?

Then, I put the mirror on the floor which showed only my ankles. I liked that a lot but it hardly helped.

Finally, I put the mirror back on the laundry basket and crouched down so I could see the top of my togs, then leapt up so I could see the middle and bottom.

Hmm. You know, with the right needlework and a bit of glue, I reckon there's another year left in that teenage two-piece...

1 Who is the target audience for this passage?

_____

2 What kind of style is the writer creating in this passage?

_____

3 This passage is written in the first person. Why?

_____

4   As this is your first passage we're going to help you out. The humorous tone/style of this article is created by using:

- amusing anecdotes
- exaggeration (hyperbole)
- alliteration
- colloquial language.

Go back to the column and, using a variety of coloured highlighters, find as many examples of the features listed above as you can.

5   Write a paragraph and, in your own words, explain why the intended audience would find this passage amusing.

_____

_____

_____

_____

_____

_____

_____

_____

_____

_____

ISBN 9780170264907

Let's go a step further ...

Here are two items from a newspaper. The first, from the *Christchurch Press,* is a news item, the second is an editorial from the *Taranaki Daily News.* They are both based around a University of Otago study on children walking to school.

We have highlighted and annotated some of the features that illustrate the difference between the two styles of writing.

Carefully read each piece and answer the questions that follow.

Fewer children go to school on foot – study

Giles Brown

The sight of children walking to school may become a thing of the past if current trends continue, a University of Otago study predicts.

A survey of 1500 Dunedin primary schoolchildren and their parents found car ownership, ethnicity and family wealth were all behind a decline in the numbers of children making the morning hike from breakfast table to classroom.

Of the children surveyed, about a third had walked to school.

A questionnaire sent out to parents revealed half of the children walked to school less than three times a week.

The director of the university's social and behavioural research unit, Dr Tony Reeder, said the study was "objective evidence" of a widely accepted trend.

The study found the number of children living further from school was a big factor in the decline.

Children living within 1km of their school were 30 times more likely to make the trip by foot than those living 3km away.

"The closure of neighbourhood schools is likely to have contributed to the reduction in the number of children who walk to school," Reeder said.

The modern car habit also drew families away from walking to school.

"We want everything quickly these days and we want to be right there right now," he said.

Children from lower socio-economic backgrounds or Pacific Island or Maori families were more likely to walk to school.

Children in schools of socio-economic deciles two and four were more than twice as likely to walk.

Boys were a third more likely to walk than girls, and Years 4 to 6 were over two-thirds more likely to walk than younger children.

Children whose parents had walked to school when they were young were over a third more likely to walk too.

Reeder said this did not mean a decline in those walking to school would see the habit disappear completely.

"I think it could without intervention, but those interventions are beginning to happen now."

The push play manager for Sport and Recreation New Zealand (Sparc), Deb Hurdle, said she thought the increasing cost of petrol might see families walk to school more often.

"People might start to think more seriously about whether they do take their car for those little journeys," she said.

Thorrington School in the Christchurch suburb of Cashmere has done its own study of walking habits.

"We really concentrated on those living within 1km and looked at targets about how many people we wanted walking to school," said principal Paul Armitage.

The number of children walking peaked at 78 per cent two weeks ago. "Children that come after having had fresh air and a little bit of exercise do come in more ready to learn."

Stepping out: a walking bus makes its way to a school. — Photo: Fairfax

Annotations:
- 3 reasons later expanded
- Statistic
- Expert
- Another significant factor
- Statistic
- Reasons why those DO walk
- Expert says in future petrol ↑, walking ↑
- Air + exercise = ready to learn

ISBN 9780170264907

TARANAKI
DAILY NEWS

Saturday, April 12, 2008

A mountain of stupidity

Editorial = opinion

Sets up a question for the reader to think 'what is this about'

IT'S remarkable just how bureaucrats and policy-wonks can get it so wrong.

Slang

Just this week we published a story about a University of Otago study that shows fewer children are walking to school.

For a variety of reasons more parents are choosing to drop their kids off in the car than let them enjoy some much-needed exercise.

Colloquial

With staggering rises in the number of obese children and adults, which some respected commentators say is a national health crisis, few children walking to their school is enough of a concern.

Emotive exaggeration

Unnamed source

But the possibility of Taranaki alpine clubs having to ditch their open mountain climbs because of bureaucratic bungling and greed is beyond belief.

Beginning with a conjunction

Cliche Slang Alliteration

Here are clubs whose members go out of their way to introduce many to our wonderful mountain, to our great outdoors, and the Department of Conservation wants to penalise them.

Repetition Personal pronoun

The department wants thousands of dollars from the clubs in permits and safety audits.

The clubs have naturally baulked at the idea and admit having to find the extra money could mean the end of climbs to the summit for hundreds of people every year, people who might otherwise be putting their feet up on the couch and preparing to climb into a mountain of TV watching. National MP Chester Borrows is bang on the money when he questions the motives of those behind the proposed levy.

Metaphor

Cliche

"DOC have forgotten who they are working for."

Quotation

Absolutely. And they have forgotten how much these groups contribute in time, effort and money towards keeping aspiring mountain-goers inspired, informed and safe.

Minor sentence

Alliteration

Without the annual open mountain climbs, people would be tempted to make the journey themselves, with all the disastrous consequences that entails.

DOC's bid for money is the wrong move at completely the wrong time and a classic example of too much red tape stopping the flow of oxygen to bureaucrats' brains.

Cliche/ metaphor

People's lives are becoming increasingly sedentary and they, and the organisations who work to inspire them off their bums and outside, should be encouraged, not actively discouraged.

Slang

Rather than having to pay for the privilege of guiding us up our great mountain, the alpine clubs and the tireless members who make up their number should be paid for the contribution they make to the greater good.

Repetition of instruction

Maybe they could take the bureaucrats and bean counters up there.

Cliche

The fresh air would help clear their heads.

ISBN 9780170264907

YOU DO:

1   These two texts are quite different in style. Explain the difference in:

• headline

_____

_____

_____

• vocabulary

_____

_____

_____

• use of expert opinion

_____

_____

_____

• use of concrete facts

_____

_____

_____

2   Why is the editorial so different from the article? Think about intended purpose and intended audience.

_____

_____

_____

_____

_____

_____

_____

_____

ISBN 9780170264907

What's next?

By now you will have some idea about how authors use different techniques to create a specific style to achieve their purpose. So, how does all this relate to you and sitting an external assessment on unfamiliar text?

Basically you need to be able to analyse a passage before you begin to answer the questions. It is a matter of being proactive rather than reactive. When you read for pleasure, you read to find out what it is all about. When you read for analysis, you have to do **more** than just read ... **you have to think at the same time**. It is not enough to read a passage for content only. You need to be alert to the techniques being used by the writer.

Here is a passage from a work of fiction, a novel. Read the passage carefully.

---

1 Over the next hundred kilometres I watched in dismay as all my determination for a new life drained away as surely as if someone had pulled the plug. I tried kidding myself it was indigestion from one-and-a-half mouthfuls of apple pie, but by the time I spotted the sign for Riverdale School, my gut was
5 churning with fear. In two days all my friends – and now I'd left them behind, they seemed so many and so brilliant – would be back in Year Thirteen at High. And here was I in the middle of nowhere, in the company of assorted farm animals, acres of grass, and a bunch of snooty girls. I longed to be in the city, fighting for a locker, grabbing a battered desk next to Daisy, yelling witty insults
10 down the stair well, sharing my cheese sandwiches and views on Life under the pohutukawa trees. It hadn't occurred to me until this minute that to start a new life you had to ditch the old one. And right now the old one felt like the most precious thing I had. But then, poor Dad, he was going back to the old life – work, garden, Gran on Sunday afternoons – the old life, but without me. And
15 without Mum. I wound down the window, trying to clear my head. I was coming to Riverdale because I'd thought it was what Dad wanted – to be on his own, to get me out of his hair. But what if he was bringing me here because he thought it was what I wanted – to get away from him? I stifled a desperate sob.
　　Dad nosed the car down a wooded drive and pulled up in front of a three
20 storey brick building smothered in ivy. There was a circular lawn in front with a statue of some pompous old bloke, and a vast spreading tree. At High the statue would have been tagged, the old bloke obscenely defaced. Here, everything was so clean and neat and classy, I already felt like an urchin in my jeans and ratty sweatshirt.

Love and Other Excuses, Jane Westaway

Before you go further ...

1 Complete the following chart.

What is it **about**?	Who is the **audience**?	What is the **style**?	What is the **purpose**?

2 Re-read the passage, and using a highlighter, highlight the different features of language you can see that the author has used. If you need help, refer back to the chart on page 12.

ISBN 9780170264907

⊢○ At this point, you are half-way there ...

You have read and analysed a passage, which is great. You have thought about it in terms of the big picture. Remember that an external assessment will require you to explain your understanding of the writer's skills and how those skills achieve the writer's purpose.

When you have made some general decisions about the text, you will move into familiar territory. All you have to do is answer the questions, just as you were taught to do in Years 9 and 10.

Having looked at the passage as a whole, you should now find the questions very straightforward to answer.

On the surface

1 What was the narrator's feeling towards the new school? Support your answer with evidence from the text.

_____

_____

_____

2 Give several pieces of information about the narrator of this passage.

_____

_____

_____

3 Give THREE examples from the passage of how Riverdale School is different from High.

Example one:

_____

_____

_____

Example two:

_____

_____

_____

Example three:

_____

_____

_____

Technical

4 Write down TWO images used in the passage and, in your own words, explain what each one means.

Image one:

_____

_____

Explanation:

_____

_____

Image two:

_____

_____

Explanation:

_____

_____

Search and think

5 In lines 15–18 the narrator has a dilemma. In your own words, explain what it is.

_____

_____

_____

6 What does the word 'pompous' in line 21 mean?

_____

_____

ISBN 9780170264907

Now let's have a look at the answers and how we got them from the passage.

1 What was the narrator's feeling towards the new school? Support your answer with evidence from the text.

The girl is sad about starting school. She doesn't want to go.

It should have been obvious that the girl is in no way positive about starting the new school. The word 'dismay' in line 1 and 'desperate sob' from line 18 tell you that the narrator is more than 'sad' about the new school. Try and think beyond short, simple words to explain yourself. Also note that this answer does not refer to the second half of the question (support your answer with evidence ...). If you do not answer the question entirely you will not succeed. This student wasted a chance at an Achieve grade.

2 Give **several** pieces of information about the narrator of this passage.

The narrator is starting a new school – Riverdale School. The narrator is female as she is going to a 'snooty' girls school. She is Y13.

The question asks for 'several' pieces of information so you should give more than two. Some of these points could be directly quoted from the text, e.g., 'back in Year Thirteen at High'. Others are inferred, e.g., about her father now being alone 'And without Mum', the country location from 'assorted farm animals' and the private school 'a bunch of snooty girls'. You would have needed to give at least two pieces of information to be awarded the grade.

3 Give **THREE** examples from the passage of how Riverdale School is different from High.

Example one:
There was no 'tagging'.

Example two:
It was 'clean, neat and classy'.

Example three:
It was in the 'country'.

This type of question tests your ability to understand what you read. In this case you needed to skim the passage and look for details that might imply differences rather than state them obviously. You would have needed three clear examples to be awarded a grade.

4   Write down **TWO** images used in the passage and, **in your own words**, explain what each one means.

Image one: '...determination for a new life drained away as surely as if someone had pulled the plug.'

Explanation: When a plug is pulled all the water disappears – this is how she sees her commitment to her change of direction in life.

Image two: 'I already felt like an urchin in my jeans and ratty sweatshirt.'

Explanation: An urchin is usually someone who lives in the street or is poor. She feels like this because everything else is so flash and 'rich'.

> An image is any picture created by words used in the passage. Always look for similes and metaphors as they are obvious. 'In your own words' means you must not repeat words already used in the passage. The marker would have expected you to get each part of this answer correct. The 'explanation' requires you to unpack the image and explain what the writer meant literally.

5   In lines 15–18 the narrator has a dilemma. **In your own words**, explain what it is.

She isn't sure if she is attending the new school because her father doesn't want her around any more OR because her father thinks she doesn't want to be living with him.

> The question directed you to certain lines from the passage. It is important that you carefully read the appropriate lines several times before you answer the question.
> The word 'dilemma' implies there is a choice to be made, therefore your answer needs two parts. Sometimes it can be tricky to rephrase the writing in the text.

6   What does the word 'pompous' in line 21 mean?

Pompous means that the person is a snob or thinks they are important.

> The question asks for a synonym (a word that has a similar meaning). It is important that you think of the context the word is being used in. See page 44 of this book.

ISBN 9780170264907

An aside on ... answering 'how' questions

We wanted to take some time to stop and look at this little word that seems to trip up a lot of students. Some of the higher level questions will begin with the phrase ... 'How does the author ...?' These are style questions. They don't ask for *what* is said i.e. the content of the text, but how the author gets the content/message across. The 'how' translates to 'what techniques did the author use to make this happen?' In these questions you must talk about techniques ... whether they be parts of speech, figures of speech, punctuation, sentence structures, vocabulary... etc.

An aside on ... answering short-answer questions

- Read the question carefully. Ensure you understand exactly what is being asked of you. If they have not already been highlighted, underline key words.
- Watch for the following phrases:

  In your own words ... this means you cannot copy straight from the text but need to reword your answer.

  Give the word ... if the question asks for a specific number of words make sure that is all you give.

  Quote part of the sentence ... quoting means you need to copy the exact words from the passage. If they ask for part of a sentence, choose only the part that answers the question. Writing the whole sentence may see you lose marks.

  In full sentences ... if you are asked for your answers to be in full sentences, do not use note form.

- If you are unsure of what answer to put down, incorporate all the information you have that relates directly to the question. That way you have covered all bases.
- The number of lines provided for the answer is a clue to how detailed your response needs to be. Try to make more than one point and give more than one example – especially if you are aiming for 'Excellence'.
- Always give a full answer – no credit is given for half an answer.
- If you have been asked to identify a poetic technique or a particular word, you must underline the specific words in the sentence you copy. This shows that you actually know the technique and have not just taken a guess. An entire phrase or sentence that includes but does not highlight the technique will not be rewarded.
- It is important that you know the terminology and can use it to explain yourself clearly.
- Many questions will allow you to score an Achieved, Merit or Excellence from your answer. A clue would be that the first thing that pops into your head is probably **NOT** the Excellence answer! Think ... mull ... expand ... quote ...

An aside on ... answering paragraph questions

When you are asked to write a paragraph answer in close reading, think about what you know from your formal writing. It's essentially the same. Make your point, explain your point and back it up with examples from the text. Then, to get that elusive Excellence, show your response to the text by explaining what you have been made to think by the passage, or what your opinion of the passage's effectiveness is. It will depend on the question, but if you can show that you have been *thinking*, you'll get better results.

ISBN 9780170264907

Written text

Call us old fashioned, but the best way for you to get better at close reading, particularly the analysis part, is to practise.

This section allows you to practise the skills that you have learnt on a variety of unfamiliar texts.

Practice text 1

Read the passage carefully.

Greasies to go ...
The search is on for the hottest fish'n'chips in the country

1   Next time you lift a chip to your trembling, anticipatory lips, pause and consider what you're about to pop into your mouth. Hold that deep-fried finger of potato up to the light and consider its heft, its colour, its confidence.

Is it a crisp and outstanding chip? Or is it a droopy, greasy, unlovable poor
5   excuse of a thing?

And what of its big friend in the golden overcoat? Is that piece of fish all it should be?

Is it fresh and white, moist and flaky? Or is it a battered soul, a snapper that has long since lost its snap, a lemon fish gone tart? And what about the batter?
10   The batter is a whole other universe.

The judges of this year's Best New Zealand Fish & Chip Shop Competition were taking the batter a bit for granted at their annual rule-setting meeting at a semi-secret meeting in central Auckland a few weeks back. But after long and often intense consideration, batter – or 'coating' as they decided to call it – was
15 given due billing in the taste-judging aspects of the contest, alongside the fish and the chips.

There are 2500 fish and chip shops in New Zealand but only one can be declared New Zealand's best. Apart from the immediate accolades, the winner can expect business to rise by 30 or 40 per cent. Or even more.
20 But the past three winners of the coveted Best Chippie (if I may abbreviate) Award weren't famous for their big servings, one of the veteran judges revealed. They were famous for the crispy nowness and tastebud-titivating qualities of their ordinary, old-fashioned fish and chips.

Last year's winner, the Westshore Fish Cafe at Bay View, north of Napier, is
25 now coping with a 50 per cent increase in business.

This year's winner is in the process of being decided by a faceless panel of judges who know their oil, their fish, their spuds and their batter, too. And they have high expectations of the things that can happen when those items are brought together with intense heat and wrapped up in paper, all crispy, and taken away for
30 instant consumption.

The competition encourages non-greasiness. In the comprehensive guide sent out to all participating shops, it instructs that thin and crinkly chips are nothing but grease traps (their phrasing is slightly different). Favour 'thick and straight', it says.
35 The judges will also consider service, variety of menu and décor as they analyse, eliminate and narrow down entrants, secretly sampling 'one scoop chips, one standard fish'.

To avoid suspicion, the judges will look like almost anyone and buy their orders at lunchtime. They'll also be looking at how they're wrapped. Double
40 wrapping is good.

ISBN 9780170264907

Before you go further ...

1 Complete the following chart.

What is it **about**?	Who is the **audience**?	What is the **style**?	What is the **purpose**?

2 Re-read the passage and, using a highlighter, select the different features of language you can see that the author has used. If you need help, refer back to the chart on page 12.

Now answer the following questions in as much detail as possible.

On the surface

1 Quote part of a sentence from lines 26-37 that shows what the judges will be sampling.

_____

_____

2 In your own words explain what the past three winners of the award were famous for.

_____

_____

3 In your own words explain why thin and crinkly chips are out of favour.

_____

_____

Technical

4 Explain the pun in the title sentence.

_____

_____

5 Why have the apostrophes been used in the phrase 'fish'n'chips' (title sentence)?

_____

_____

6 Find an example of a metaphor in lines 1-10.

_____

7 'The batter is a whole other universe' (line 10) is an example of what language feature?

_____

8 Comment on the sentence structure of lines 6-10, 'And what of its ... whole other universe.'

_____

_____

9 Why has the word 'coating' (line 14) been placed in inverted commas?

_____

_____

10 Why have brackets been used in the following sentence? 'But the past three winners of the coveted Best Chippie (if I may abbreviate) Award weren't famous for their big servings, one of the veteran judges revealed.'

_____

_____

11 The word 'greasies' (title), 'chippie' (line 20) and 'spuds' (line 27) are examples of what language style?

_____

12 Explain what a compound word is and list TWO examples from the passage.

_____

_____

Search and think

13 Why are the judges considered to be 'faceless'?

_____

_____

_____

_____

_____

COMMENT...
EXPLAIN...
DESCRIBE...
At this level these generally mean the same thing:
write about it.

You might have noticed that there are no grades attached to the questions in this book.
WHY?
Because at this stage you are learning the skills of close reading, rather than worrying about the final grade.

ISBN 9780170264907

Practice text 2

Read the passage carefully.

Routeburn

1 'This place is turning into a suburban walkway,' lamented the grey-bearded man
next to me. 'A few more years, mate, and they won't have to maintain this track –
they'll sweep it!'

From our vantage point high above Harris Saddle, the alpine section of the
5 Routeburn Track sprawled before us like a highway, shimmering in December heat.
Brightly coloured centipedes of walkers passed each other along the trail and
wrapped themselves around the brown steel Harris Saddle shelter shaped like a
miniature airport hangar. Someone yodelled, and the tussock meadows rippled
with laughter and more or less successful imitations. My companion, an old-
10 fashioned Kiwi tramper dressed in blue-checked Swanndri and green rugby shorts,
snorted in disgust. He hadn't walked the track for 20 years, and what he saw now
wasn't tramping as he knew it.

The 39-kilometre-long Routeburn straddles the spine of the Humboldt
Mountains, which mark the border between Fiordland and Mount Aspiring National
15 Parks. It is the busiest transalpine artery in New Zealand, and yet, some say,
still the most beautiful. Whether a result of slick advertising or word of mouth
over pizza and cheap wine at backpackers' hostels, its popularity has reached
astonishing proportions.

Every year the Routeburn attracts more than 10,000 visitors. They burn seven
20 tonnes of coal and 2000 kg of gas, use nearly 3000 rolls of toilet paper and keep
six seasonal staff frantically busy. In summer, the car parks at both ends of the
track can resemble parking lots of a good-size supermarket as scores of trampers
and day-walkers window-shop for nature's treasures.

Despite their strong outdoors tradition, New Zealanders make up only a quarter
25 of the total number of visitors. Promoted as a major destination by the tourism
industry, the Routeburn has become so dominated by foreigners that local
trampers are beginning to feel like strangers in their own backyard.

And that backyard is starting to show a few cracks. Local or foreign,
thoughtful and nature-loving as they might be, the walkers have brought
30 problems: overcrowded huts, illegal camping, rubbish and the threat of giardia.
Most of all, they have endangered the elusive sense of wilderness, the very reason
for their visit.

The heart of the problem is that the boom in visitor numbers – in all the
35 national parks, not just Fiordland – has not been matched by government
expenditure to maintain and improve facilities. It is only the tolerance of visitors
and the ingenuity of track staff which have kept the Routeburn functioning more
or less successfully. Now, as demand for the Routeburn and her sister tracks
continues to increase, new ways of managing the human torrent are being put
40 in place.

New Zealand Geographic

ISBN 9780170264907

Before you go further ...

1 Complete the following chart.

What is it **about**?	Who is the **audience**?	What is the **style**?	What is the **purpose**?

2 Re-read the passage and, using a highlighter, select the different features of language you can see that the author has used. If you need help, refer back to the chart on page 12.

Answer the following questions in as much detail as possible.

On the surface

1 Why does the Routeburn track resemble 'a surburban walkway' (line 1)?

_____

_____

2 How has the track's popularity grown?

_____

_____

_____

3 Why do local trampers feel like strangers?

_____

_____

_____

4 List FIVE problems caused by the visitors.

_____

_____

_____

_____

_____

_____

_____

ISBN 9780170264907

Technical

5 Explain the metaphor 'centipedes of walkers' (line 6).

_____

_____

6 How is the Routeburn Track compared with the human body? (paragraph 3)

_____

_____

_____

7 The writer uses a metaphor to suggest that numbers of visitors are overwhelming. What is the metaphor?

_____

_____

_____

Search and think

8 Explain what 'that backyard' (line 29) is referring to.

_____

_____

_____

9 In your own words explain how the writer has used both information and emotion in the passage to convey his ideas.

_____

_____

_____

_____

You will notice that from now on, the questions are no longer divided into three sections for you because Year 11 assessment will be a mixture of these question types.

Practice text 3

Read the passage carefully. It is the beginning of a magazine article written about Sam Morgan before he sold Trade Me.

Hello. My name is Mike and I'm a recovering Trade Me addict.

In the last 12 months I've bought a designer coffee pot, two kayaks, a VW Barbie, a pair of ski boots, a Che Guevara box, a spice grinder, a Thunderbirds 2 torch and an orange bikini.

I was doing fine until recently when I bought a Vespa fridge magnet. Okay, two of them.

I now realise I'm not completely safe on my own with a laptop and Trade Me link. But I know there are thousands of others like me out there, battling the same sin.

And I also know the guy who's to blame.

His name's Sam Morgan, he's sharp, smart, probably pretty rich and only 29. What he started in his bedroom is now shared by a million New Zealanders. Trade Me is an internet site where people put things up for sale and others bid for it. It's simple, free and anyone on a computer can get involved. Stuff for sale can be new or used, from a baby's bib to an Auckland apartment, a moped to a Maserati.

It's called an online auction site but this isn't about number babbling and gavel whacking. It's more the 21st century version of the garage sale, a church jumble sale somewhere in cyberspace. It's become New Zealand's busiest website (with 20 million traders predicted this year).

And the country's fastest-growing company, according to the last Deloitte Fast 50 survey – revenue screaming up by 1200 per cent over the last two years, like a Lamborghini with the clutch dropped.

Sam Morgan doesn't flinch at the numbers any more. The exponential upwards sweep of users, sales and revenue has been pure accountancy aerobatics, staggering increase upon staggering increase.

But go to find Morgan and you won't enter a world of chrome and Gucci. The lift to Trade Me central in a Stalinesque Wellington office block lumbers like a Lada, heavy doors heaving open to reveal Trade Me signage and not a lot else. No faux-blonde secretary chirrups 'How may I help you?' because there's no reception desk – just a display of auction paraphernalia, including a Starsky and Hutch cap, a paint-by-numbers version of Van Gogh's Sunflowers, some false eyelashes and a 45 of Mario Lanza rumbling Christmas carols.

There's no nameplate on a smoked glass door saying General Manager because Morgan doesn't have an office. In a sea of corporate youth, he sits in the middle of 40 other workers in scrunched tee shirt and Levis. His number two haircut betrays a ginger tinge, while fading freckles and unconvincing stubble betray his age.

He says 'wicked … cool …. sweet' and it doesn't jar like it would from your average crusty company head.

Before you go further ...

1 Complete the following chart.

What is it **about**?	Who is the **audience**?	What is the **style**?	What is the **purpose**?

2 Re-read the passage and, using a highlighter, select the different features of language you can see that the author has used. If you need help refer back to the chart on page 12.

Answer the following questions in as much detail as possible.

1 Why does the article begin with the 'handwritten' words? Does the article continue this style?

_____

_____

_____

2 Find TWO examples of similes that use a car image. Explain why they are effective.

_____

_____

_____

_____

3 Using information from paragraphs 4,5 and 6 explain how the writer knows Sam Morgan is not the typical corporate businessman.

_____

_____

_____

_____

_____

_____

4 What is the writer's attitude towards Sam Morgan and his business? Select TWO phrases that show this attitude.

_____

_____

_____

_____

_____

ISBN 9780170264907

sunday service

so gay

Steve Braunias explores a strange new slander among our nation's kids

Mr and Mrs Beckham, parents of three: so gay
PHOTOGRAPH: AFP

Reading is gay. Maths is gay. The headmaster is totally gay. Morning playtime is gay and so is the food your parents give you for lunch. That dumb shirt – gay. Those awful shoes – gay. Little sisters? Gay. Little brothers? So gay that they may as well be little sisters. Parents do their best, but the plain fact of the matter is that Mum and Dad – inevitable, really, with their nagging and their appalling ignorance of the best things in life – are almost always gay.

Gay is the new insult, the new slander among our nation's kids. How new? Actually, it's kind of old. It seems to have crept into New Zealand about four, five years ago, and has since spread across intermediate schools like moss. It's also in use at primary school and college, but the word peaks with kids aged 11-13. "That's so gay," they announce. "Soooooo gay".

By gay, the mean: lame, stupid, uncool, false, wrong, useless, idiotic, irrelevant, phoney. To be gay is to be rewarded with the highest scorn and contempt. More intelligent users will horse around with the word; for example, "Mr Morris is the ultimate in gay technology." Or: "The gaiety of the speech by Mr Morris was overwhelming." Studies, incidentally, show that most people called Morris are so gay.

What a curious business. Why have they latched onto that particular term? In the lexicon of the 12-year-old New Zealander, gay no longer means gay. They have stripped the word of its sexuality. Really, they have stripped the word of this power.

Gay pride, gay rights, gay lifestyle – that means nothing any more. The gay movement, which worked so hard to find a place in mainstream life, has been stopped in its tracks by brats. They have put a whoopee cushion under it, subverted it, given it another shape.

Why has it taken such particular hold with kids that age? The fact is that no one

can identify what's lame, stupid, uncool, false, wrong, useless, idiotic, irrelevant, and phoney with the accuracy and daring of a 12-year-old. Teenagers are too busy posing; adults are past it. At 12, you occupy a state of grace. Childhood, with its giddiness and its toys, is over. The noise of adolesencebangs like a distant drum. At 12, you are in-between – literally, at an intermediate stage.

The body is in revolt, but even more tumultuous change is taking place in the brain, because 12 is the age with the brain makes it debut. A 12-year-old mind is as shiny as a new coin. It flips in the air and makes an instant judgement call – it can tell in a flash what or who is and is not so gay.

Most celebrities are so gay. David Beckham is so gay. Tom Cruise is so gay. Paris Hilton is so gay. In New Zealand, Matthew Ridge, Paul Holmes and Nicky Watson are so gay. The kids know these things. At 12, they are gifted with fabulous insight. Their convictions are strong, their faith is infinite. They have so few distractions. No one takes them seriously. They can't drive, they can't drink. Sex is a private affair. Homework, which is gay, hardly takes up much of their time – they are unburdened by the pressure of crucial exams. Essentially, they are left alone, half-human, half-savage, quite pure.

All well and good, and please excuse the rampant stereotyping of children aged 12. But what to make of the choice of the word gay? It almost certainly arrived on our shores from the US. American online magazine Salon ran a story about it back in 2000. Seven years ago, according to the report, the term was used among adults; Salon argued that it merely

"evoked childhood", and was entirely innocent, something to be encouraged.

Really? Last month, the term came before a judge in California. When classmates teased a 13-year-old schoolgirl about her Mormon upbringing ("Do you have 10 moms?"), she responded with the withering put-down: "That's so gay". The principal gave the girl an official warning. Her parents have sued the school. They say the warning has violated her First Amendment rights. They are also – this is so gay – seeking "unspecified damages." The school says the girl was using hate speech. Its lawyers told the court, "We have a duty to protect gay students from harassment … In furtherance of this goal, prohibition of the phrase 'That's so gay' was a reasonable regulation." The judge will make her ruling next month.

Only in America, probably. But in prim, anxious New Zealand, the use of the term is waiting for trouble. Actually, it has already attracted a complaint to the Broadcasting Standards Authority. Last year, a kid on TV One programme Top of the Class announced that playing the recorder was "extremely gay". Paul Davies complained, saying it would encourage kids to think "gay is bad". The authority ruled that it didn't breach broadcasting standards.

Soon, though, gay will be the old black. Language picks up, discards, moves on. A new expression of scorn and contempt will be needed and seized on without adult supervision or approval. It could well be that anyone lame, stupid, uncool etc will wake up one day in the near future and hear the withering put-down: "You're so het."

Email: stephen.b@star-times.co.nz

ISBN 9780170264907

Before you go further ...

1 Complete the following chart.

What is it **about**?	Who is the **audience**?	What is the **style**?	What is the **purpose**?

2 Re-read the passage and, using a highlighter, select the different features of language you can see that the author has used. If you need help, refer back to the chart on page 12.

Answer the following questions in as much detail as possible. Tackle the three basic questions first, which should expand on what you have written in the grid above.

1 What is the subject of this article?

_____

_____

_____

2 Who is the audience?

_____

_____

_____

3 What is the style of the writing?

_____

_____

_____

Now go on to examine how the writer achieves these outcomes. Answer these next two questions about the passage.

4 Look at the opening paragraph of the article. What techniques have the writer and the magazine used to gain the reader's attention?

_____

_____

_____

_____

_____

_____

_____

5 Find one example of a simile, a metaphor, three examples of colloquial language, one example of irony and two examples of hyperbole used in the writing. Explain the effect of each technique.

Simile: _____

Effect: _____

Metaphor: _____

Effect: _____

Colloquial language (x3): _____

Effect: _____

Irony: _____

Effect: _____

Hyperbole: _____

Effect: _____

Finally, think about the author's opinion, and your own opinion.

6 Does the writer care about the way the word 'gay' is being used? What does he predict will happen to the word?

_____

_____

_____

_____

_____

_____

7 What do you think about this topic? Have you used the word in this way? Do you still? Should we be worried about the way the meaning of words is changing?

_____

_____

_____

_____

_____

ISBN 9780170264907

Practice text 5

Read the passage carefully. This extract is the opening of a novel. It sets a scene and introduces a character. As this is a more complex text, we are going to help by annotating the passage. These highlights, notes and comments are what your teacher would be discussing with you about the passage.

Annotations (left margin):

- Setting Personification Use of comma makes you pause, go slowly over the o sounds.
- Onomatopoeia
- Baffled with vacuously: sense of pointless life?
- One sentence paragraph. Alliteration. Sense of foreboding.
- Alliteration. Quicker pace than opening para. Thrilled = emotive
- Short sentences again add detail
- Verbs: action Laterite = reddish clay
- Introduces a character. Tense changed. From always to this particular time.
- Alliteration, Metaphor, Simile, Physical verb – slammed
- In contrast
- Minor sentence
- Repetition of still. Links to Rahel coming *back*.

Annotations (right margin):

- Metaphor, Contrast, Emotive language: gorge, dustgreen
- Short sentences create images.
- Words to look up: dissolute (overindulging, harming oneself), vacuously (pointless, unintelligent).
- Fruity sums up previous words.
- Immodest? (exposing things usually covered). New growth appearing everywhere, not hidden.
- Metaphor - visual
- Begins with a conjunction – why? Final sentence of description.
- Personification
- Descriptive detail
- Onomatopoeia
- Next 3 expand on first sentence.
- Explains previous sentence more.

From *The God of Small Things,* by Arundhati Roy
Paradise Pickles and Preserves

May in Ayemenem is a hot, brooding month. The days are long and humid. The river shrinks and black crows gorge on bright mangoes in still, dustgreen trees. Red bananas ripen. Jackfruit burst. Dissolute bluebottles hum vacuously in the fruity air. Then they stun themselves against clear windowpanes and die, fatly baffled in the sun.

The nights are clear but suffused with sloth and sullen expectation.

But by early June the south-west monsoon breaks and there are three months of wind and water with short spells of sharp glittering sunshine that thrilled children snatch to play with. The countryside turns an immodest green. Boundaries blur as tapioca fences take root and bloom. Brick walls turn mossgreen. Pepper vines snake up electric poles. Wild creepers burst through laterite banks and spill across the flooded roads. Boats ply in the bazaars. And small fish appear in the puddles that fill the PWD potholes on the highways.

It was raining when Rahel came back to Ayemenem. Slanting silver ropes slammed into loose earth, ploughing it up like gunfire. The old house on the hill wore its steep, gabled roof pulled over its ears like a low hat. The walls streaked with moss, had grown soft, and bulged a little with dampness that seeped up from the ground.

The wild, overgrown garden was full of the whisper and scurry of small lives. In the undergrowth a rat snake rubbed itself against a glistening stone. Hopeful bullfrogs cruised the scummy pond for mates. A drenched mongoose flashed across the leaf-strewn driveway.

The house itself looked empty. The doors and windows were locked. The front verandah bare. Unfurnished. But the skyblue Plymouth with chrome tailfins was still parked outside, and inside, Baby Kochamma was still alive.

Before you go further …

1 Complete the following chart.

What is it **about**?	Who is the **audience**?	What is the **style**?	What is the **purpose**?

2 Re-read the passage and, using a highlighter, select the different features of language you can see that the author has used. If you need help, refer back to the chart on page 12.

Answer the following questions in as much detail as possible.

1 In your own words, describe the scene set by the opening paragraph. Discuss some of the techniques the writer has used to create this scene. Is it an effective opening?

_____

_____

_____

2 The third paragraph deals with a different month. How does the writer show the differences between May and June?

_____

_____

_____

3 Choose an effective figure of speech that you have not mentioned so far, and explain why it is effective.

_____

_____

_____

4 Choose a part of speech that you have not mentioned so far, and explain why it is effective.

_____

_____

5 In paragraph 4 the tense changes. How? Why?

_____

_____

_____

ISBN 9780170264907

6 Which words in paragraphs 4 and 5 tell you that Rahel has been here before?

_____

_____

_____

7 How does the beginning of paragraph 5 contrast with what has been said in paragraph 4?

_____

_____

_____

An aside on ... emotive language

Emotive language is the deliberate use of words to exaggerate, describing a subject or an event to interest the reader or listener in a way that will excite the emotions.

Emotive words are used extensively in persuasive writing and speaking to convince others of an author's point of view, often on a controversial issue. They express bias, a tendency towards a particular point of view or preference.

There are many examples of emotive language in today's print media and in advertising e.g. controversial headlines in newspapers or suggestive ones in women's magazines, political writing that captures the opinion of the electorate, persuasive letters to the editor, or charity appeals. Talkback radio callers with strong opinions often use highly emotive language, too.

Ordinary word	Emotive word/s	Try to think of some more emotive ways of saying:
Changed	transformed, mutated, revolutionised	Injured _____
Actor	celebrity, star, ham	Light _____
Old person	elder, pensioner, kuia, senior citizen	Sad _____
Killed	slaughtered, put to sleep, euthanased	Thin _____
Fire	blaze, inferno, conflagration, bonfire	Intelligent _____

YOU DO:

John Key, as Leader of the National Party, wrote this emotive item to express one political party's views in the newspaper. We have selected some of his emotive words for you to think about. Look up any you do not know the meaning of, 'draconian' and 'travesty' for example.

National opposes this **self-serving** and **draconian** bill because it is an **assault** on democracy and free speech in election year.

The legislation widens the regulated election period to an **outrageous** one year in three, so when New Zealanders wake up on January 1 they will be regulated by election campaign rules. It **treats New Zealanders as if they are stupid** and seeks to **shut down** opposing opinion in election year.

It imposes a **shambolic** set of rules that nobody, not even Government ministers, the Prime Minister, nor the agency charged with administering it understands. It imposes a **ridiculous and unworkable** third-party regime on anyone who isn't an MP. And it lets Labour spend **tens of millions** of taxpayer dollars through government department advertising in election year to promote Labour policies and **buy** the election.

In summary, it **screws the scrum** in Labour's favour in election year because it is all about shutting down dissent and getting Labour re-elected. Labour **does not care** that our ability to speak freely and engage in political debate is the **casualty**.

The bill is an **anti-democratic travesty** that attacks the rights of ordinary New Zealanders, because their rights no longer count under a government desperate to win another term. National will **axe** this legislation at the first opportunity.

Clearly the writer is not happy. You will get the message even more clearly if you try reading it aloud with emotion!

ISBN 9780170264907

⊷O Poetry

We know that some students really love reading and understanding poetry. We also know that others see a poem more as a crossword puzzle to figure out, and a few even think a poem is something the school's English Department invented to make life difficult for teenagers.

Get over it ☺

At least poems are usually quite short and so you can focus easily on one for a brief time to understand and appreciate it.

We hope that you will find the poems we offer here help you to work out effective ways of approaching other poems given to you to study this year. Your teacher is there to help you – as well as those students in your class who enjoy poetry.

In the past you have probably done a fair bit of labelling techniques that a poet has used in a poem. You may have begun to consider why the poet used those techniques. It is now time, in Year 11, to bring it all together and to look at the poem as a whole and to look at its style.

You have been taken through the process of approaching a poem in Year 9 and 10. If you need a refresher course then go back to pages 54-60 in *How to ... Achieve in Year 9* or pages 56-59 in *How to ... Achieve in Year 10*.

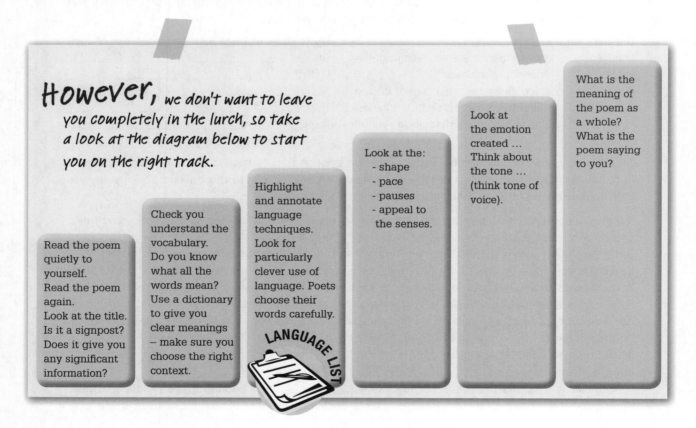

However, we don't want to leave you completely in the lurch, so take a look at the diagram below to start you on the right track.

Read the poem quietly to yourself.
Read the poem again.
Look at the title. Is it a signpost? Does it give you any significant information?

Check you understand the vocabulary. Do you know what all the words mean? Use a dictionary to give you clear meanings – make sure you choose the right context.

LANGUAGE LIST

Highlight and annotate language techniques. Look for particularly clever use of language. Poets choose their words carefully.

Look at the:
- shape
- pace
- pauses
- appeal to the senses.

Look at the emotion created ... Think about the tone ... (think tone of voice).

What is the meaning of the poem as a whole? What is the poem saying to you?

ISBN 9780170264907

Let's work together first ...

This poem has been annotated for you to draw your attention to some of its features.

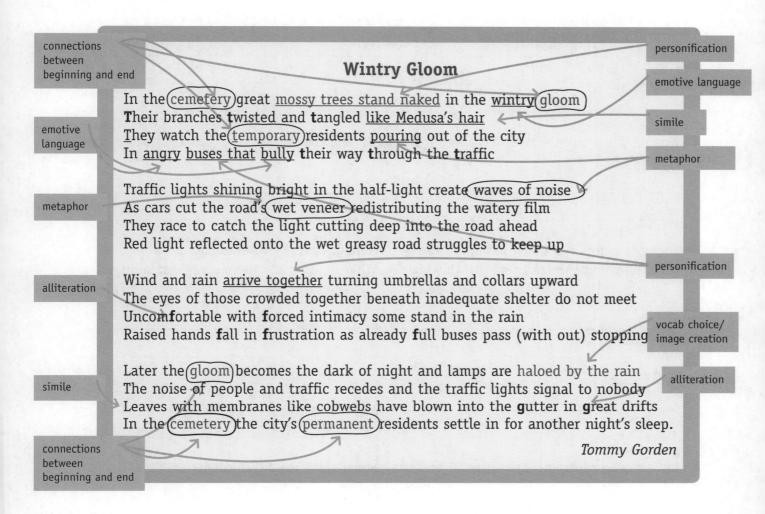

Wintry Gloom

connections between beginning and end

personification

emotive language

simile

In the (cemetery) great mossy trees stand naked in the wintry (gloom)
Their branches **t**wisted and **t**angled like Medusa's hair
They watch the (temporary) residents pouring out of the city
In angry buses that bully **t**heir way **t**hrough the **t**raffic

emotive language

metaphor

metaphor

Traffic lights shining bright in the half-light create (waves of noise)
As cars cut the road's (wet veneer) redistributing the watery film
They race to catch the light cutting deep into the road ahead
Red light reflected onto the wet greasy road struggles to keep up

personification

alliteration

Wind and rain arrive together turning umbrellas and collars upward
The eyes of those crowded together beneath inadequate shelter do not meet
Uncom**f**ortable with **f**orced intimacy some stand in the rain
Raised hands **f**all in **f**rustration as already **f**ull buses pass (with out) stopping

vocab choice/ image creation

simile

Later the (gloom) becomes the dark of night and lamps are haloed by the rain
The noise of people and traffic recedes and the traffic lights signal to nobody
Leaves with membranes like cobwebs have blown into the **g**utter in **g**reat drifts
In the (cemetery) the city's (permanent) residents settle in for another night's sleep.

alliteration

connections between beginning and end

Tommy Gorden

We've helped with the analysis. Now your task is to answer a few questions in as much detail as possible.

1   This New Zealand poem is very descriptive. The poet is asking you to imagine this city scene. Either list the things that you can see, or draw a picture, if you prefer.

ISBN 9780170264907

2 Some punctuation has been left out altogether. Read the poem aloud and put in punctuation marks where you think they are needed.

Now let's look at some of the language chosen by the poet.

3 In the opening line, how does the writer suggest the cemetery is an old place?

_____

_____

_____

4 Why do you think the poet has chosen the simile 'branches twisted and tangled like Medusa's hair'?

_____

_____

5 The poet paints a detailed picture of the wet evening. Choose two examples of personification that add detail to this picture. What do they add to your understanding?

_____

_____

_____

_____

_____

_____

6 Explain who the 'temporary' (line 3) and the 'permanent' (line 16) residents are.

_____

_____

_____

_____

7 What is the central theme of this poem?

_____

_____

_____

_____

ISBN 9780170264907

Let's make a comparison ...

Wintry Gloom is a modern poem describing a winter evening in a city. The next poem was written over a hundred years ago on exactly the same subject. The poet is describing a winter's evening in the early part of the 20th century. You will note that he mentions a cab-horse which tells you the poem is set in the days before buses.

> From **Preludes**
> The winter evening settles down
> With smells of steaks in passageways.
> Six o'clock.
> The burnt-out ends of smoky days.
> And now a gusty shower wraps
> The grimy scraps
> Of withered leaves about your feet
> And newspapers from vacant lots;
> The showers beat
> On broken blinds and chimney-pots
> And at the corner of the street
> A lonely cab-horse steams and stamps.
> And then the lighting of the lamps.
>
> *T.S. Eliot*

This poem has a firmly controlled rhythm (count the syllables in the lines to see).

8 Although this poem is set in a car-less era, can you see any similarities in the way T.S. Eliot and Tommy Gorden see a winter evening in the city?

_____

_____

_____

_____

9 What do the following phrases mean to you?

a burnt-out ends _____

_____

b smoky days _____

_____

c withered leaves _____

_____

d broken blinds _____

_____

e lonely cab-horse _____

_____

10 How does T.S. Eliot feel about city life, do you think?

_____

_____

_____

_____

_____

_____

An aside on ... context

It is important to understand that to succeed at this level you will now be expected to answer questions in the context of the whole passage.

Context means the words, phrases and passages that come before and after the words you are being asked about.

For example, it will no longer be enough to just identify a simile and explain that it is comparing two things. You will now need to explain the nature of the simile's point of comparison and relate that comparison to the whole piece.

Let's look at an example. The poet is describing his vessel:

*'As idle as a painted ship
Upon a painted ocean'*

- We could say the poet is using a simile, comparing his ship to a picture of a ship.
- We could go further and say that the poet is suggesting that the ship is not moving at all.
- Or we could link the idea to the poem (*The Rime of the Ancient Mariner,* by Samuel Taylor Coleridge) as a whole and say that the poet is showing the reader how the mariner feels trapped and powerless on this ship that is supposed to carry him along but is not moving at all, as trapped as if he were on a ship in a painting.

You should be ready to have a go on your own now. Complete the following four practice tasks. You will notice that each poem has been placed on the page so that there is space for you to write your own observations around the poem. Use the boxes to help you. In other words, annotate the poem before you attempt to answer the questions.

ISBN 9780170264907

Use a dictionary to look up the following words:

Bric-a-brac	terrapin	potto
myna	bicker	neutered
dowagers	macaw	succubus
whim		

Underline any phrases you think are significant. Underline any language techniques you come across. Think about why the poet used them ... what do they add to the image, poem, your understanding?

Pet Shop

Cold blood or warm, crawling or fluttering
Bric-a-brac, all are here to be bought,
Noisy or silent, python or myna,
Fish with long silk trains like dowagers,
Monkeys lost to thought.   5

In a small tank tiny enameled
Green terrapin jostle, in a cage a crowd
Of small birds elbow each other and bicker
While beyond the ferrets, eardrum, eyeball
Find that macaw too loud.   10

Here behind glass lies a miniature desert,
The sand littered with rumpled gauze
Discarded by snakes like used bandages;
In the next door desert fossilized lizards
Stand in a pose, a pause.   15

But most of the customers want something comfy –
Rabbit, hamster, potto, puss –
Something to hold on the lap and cuddle
Making believe it will return affection
Like some neutered succubus.   20

Purr then or chirp, you are here for our pleasure,
Here at the mercy of our whim and purse;
Once there was the wild, now tanks and cages,
But we can offer you a home, a haven,
That might prove even worse.   25

Louis MacNeice

Answer the following questions in as much detail as possible.

1   In the first 15 lines of the poem the poet creates an atmosphere of a crowded, well stocked, busy pet shop. How has he done this?

_____

_____

_____

_____

_____

2   Explain what the poet means in each of the following:

a   Bric-a-brac, all are here to be bought (line 2)

_____

_____

b   Fish with long silk trains like dowagers (line 4)

_____

_____

c   Monkeys lost to thought (line 5)

_____

_____

d   ... eardrum, eyeball
    Find that macaw too loud (lines 9/10)

_____

_____

e   The sand littered with rumpled gauze
    Discarded by snakes like used bandages (lines 12/13)

_____

_____

3   The writer's attitude to pet shops comes out in the last stanza of the poem. Explain why he thinks people buy pets and what you think his attitude is to this.

_____

_____

_____

_____

ISBN 9780170264907

Use a dictionary to look up the following words:

Stippled   resound
frigid   rata
papa

Underline any phrases you think are significant. Underline any language techniques you come across. Think about why the poet used them ... what do they add to the image, poem, your understanding?

Grief on the Whanganui River

Water; calm, rippled, rain stippled,
is a mirror reaching from
the frigid mountains to the sea.
Steep papa cliffs, speckled shell-rock
willow boughs, ferns   5
stare up from the water.
Waterfalls, rapids,
bursts of bird-song resound
and all the while
the bushclad land stands proud   10
in a cloak of red rata.
It towers above travelers
hopes they'll understand
for here, the red of the rata
means battles, bloodshed, bitterness   15
on river and land.

Anne McDonnell

Answer the following questions in as much detail as possible.

1 What is the poet describing in the first 8 lines of the poem?

_____

_____

_____

2 What image is created in lines 10-11?

_____

_____

_____

3 Comment on the use of alliteration in line 15.

_____

_____

_____

4 Contrast the beginning and end of the poem. Why has the poet chosen to show this difference?

_____

_____

_____

5 Comment on the title of the poem. In your opinion, is it an effective title?

_____

_____

_____

ISBN 9780170264907

Underline any phrases you think are significant. Underline any language techniques you come across. Think about why the poet used them ... what do they add to the image, poem, your understanding?

Being Sixteen

It's
Never been easy
Sixteening:
Reading Shakespeare,
Searching for meaning;   5
Playing different roles
For everyone you've met
Wanting all the applause
You can get.

Feeling guilty   10
For deeds not done:
Trying to connect with anyone:
Searching for words
With crystal-clear meaning:
Never been easy   15
Sixteening.

A head that's full
Of new dreams every week,
Like treetops that trap
Morning mist off a creek: 20
Pushing out feelers
And pulling them in:
Trying to be yourself
While still fitting in:
Standing tall   25
When your heart's bleeding:
Never been easy
Sixteening.

Michael Khan

Answer the following questions in as much detail as possible.

1 The poet chooses to turn 'Being Sixteen' into a verb 'Sixteening'. Can you think why he has done so?

_____

_____

_____

2 Explain these two metaphors in as much detail as possible:

a 'Pushing out feelers/And pulling them in' (lines 21/22)

_____

_____

_____

b 'Standing tall/When your heart's bleeding' (lines 25/26)

_____

_____

_____

3 The poet selects several other things that make life complicated for sixteen-year-olds. What are they? Try to use your own words.

_____

_____

_____

4 Do you agree with the poet? Do you disagree? Why? Explain in detail.

_____

_____

_____

_____

_____

_____

ISBN 9780170264907

Use a dictionary to look up the following words:
docile   animate
tethered   terrestrial

Underline any phrases you think are significant. Underline any language techniques you come across. Think about why the poet used them ... what do they add to the image, poem, your understanding?

Kite

On the beach the waves pour in furiously
The wind lashes the dunes
The bay fills with rain, smoky, and clears
And from the hill's bulk the flax bushes
Shine out suddenly, like many waterfalls.   5

So fly the yellow kite, a brave flutter
Against the grey and brown. It bucks and
Dives, pulling down hope from the sky.
Behind, the thirty-foot scarlet tail snaps
In the wind, a red scissor of light.   10

It is a live thing, tugging
At the end of its lines. It is not docile
Like the purple and green dragon kite
Content to sit all day, bobbing as the breeze
Drops and lifts, tethered to the fence.   15

It cruises, hungry
Very small and spare, animate, fierce
Its one black eye regarding us curiously
Two grayish brown figures, heavy
Terrestrial, shoes full of sand.   20

Anne French

ISBN 9780170264907

Answer the following questions in as much detail as possible.

1 Emotive words are used in verse 1 to describe the weather. Identify effective words and comment on their use.

_____

_____

_____

_____

_____

2 What does the poet want the reader to notice about the kite in verse 2?

_____

_____

_____

3 Verse 3 compares the yellow kite with another kite. Explain how the poet sees this other kite.

_____

_____

_____

_____

4 In verse 4 the poet describes the yellow kite as if it is alive, with an eye to watch the people on the beach. What is the meaning of this verse?

_____

_____

_____

_____

_____

_____

ISBN 9780170264907

Playing with poetry

Read this famous poem through carefully several times. It's a very good one to read aloud or have read to you. Notice the rhyme and the rhythm. It is called a **narrative poem** because it tells a story.

The Lady of Shalott

Part I

On either side the river lie
Long fields of barley and of rye,
That clothe the wold and meet the sky;
And through the field the road runs by
    To many-towered Camelot;
And up and down the people go,
Gazing where the lilies blow
Round an island there below,
    The island of Shalott.

Willows whiten, aspens quiver,
Little breezes dusk and shiver
Through the wave that runs for ever
By the island in the river
    Flowing down to Camelot.
Four grey walls, and four grey towers
Overlook a space of flowers,
And the silent isle imbowers
    The Lady of Shalott.

> repetition
> the prison colour, captive apart from the world

By the margin, willow veiled
Slide the heavy barges trailed
By slow horses; and unhailed
The shallop flitteth silken-sailed
    Skimming down to Camelot;
But who hath seen her wave her hand?
Or at the casement seen her stand?
Or is she known in all the land,
    The Lady of Shalott?

> she is a mystery, makes no contact with world rhetorical question

Only reapers, reaping early
In among the bearded barley,
Hear a song that echoes cheerly
From the river winding clearly,
    Down to towered Camelot;
And by the moon the reaper weary,
Piling sheaves in uplands airy,
Listening, whispers 'Tis the fairy
    Lady of Shalott.'

Part II

There she weaves by night and day
A magic web with colours gay.
She has heard a whisper say,
A curse is on her if she stay
    To look down to Camelot.
She knows not what the curse may be,
And so she weaveth steadily,
And little other care hath she,
    The Lady of Shalott.

And moving through a mirror clear
That hangs before her all the year,
Shadows of the world appear.
There she sees the highway near
    Winding down to Camelot;
There the river eddy whirls,
And there the surly village-churls,
And the red cloaks of market girls,
    Pass onward from Shalott.

Sometimes a troop of damsels glad,
An abbot on an ambling pad,
Sometimes a curly shepherd-lad,
Or long-haired page in crimson clad,
    Goes by to towered Camelot;
And sometimes through the mirror blue
The knights come riding two and two:
She hath no loyal knight and true,
    The Lady of Shalott.

But in her web she still delights
To weave the mirror's magic sights,
For often through the silent nights
A funeral, with plumes and lights
    And music, went to Camelot;
Or when the moon was overhead,
Came two young lovers lately wed;
'I am half sick of shadows,' said
    The Lady of Shalott.

Part III

A bow-shot from her bower-eaves,
He rode between the barley-sheaves,
The sun came dazzling through the leaves,
And flamed upon the brazen greaves
    Of bold Sir Lancelot.
A red-cross knight for ever kneeled
To a lady in his shield,

That sparkled in the yellow field,
　　Beside remote Shalott.

The gemmy bridle glittered free,
Like to some branch of stars we see
Hung in the golden Galaxy.
The bridle bells rang merrily
　　As he rode down to Camelot;
And from his blazoned baldric slung
A mighty silver bugle hung,
And as he rode his armour rung,
　　Beside remote Shalott.

All in the blue unclouded weather
Thick-jewelled shone the saddle-leather,
The helmet and the helmet-feather
Burned like one burning flame together,
　　As he rode down to Camelot;
As often through the purple night,
Below the starry clusters bright,
Some bearded meteor, trailing light,
　　Moves over still Shalott.

His broad clear brow in sunlight glowed;
On burnished hooves his war-horse trode;
From underneath his helmet flowed
His coal-black curls as on he rode,
　　As he rode down to Camelot.
From the bank and from the river
He flashed into the crystal mirror,
'Tirra lirra,' by the river
　　Sang Sir Lancelot.

She left the web, she left the loom,
She made three paces through the room,
She saw the water-lily bloom,
She saw the helmet and the plume,
　　She looked down to Camelot.
Out flew the web and floated wide;
The mirror cracked from side to side;
'The curse is come upon me,' cried
　　The Lady of Shalott.

Part IV
In the stormy east-wind straining,
The pale yellow woods were waning,
The broad stream in his banks complaining,
Heavily the low sky raining
　　Over towered Camelot;
Down she came and found a boat
Beneath a willow left afloat,
And round about the prow she wrote
　　The Lady of Shalott.

And down the river's dim expanse
Like some bold seer in a trance,
Seeing all his own mischance —
With a glassy countenance
　　Did she look to Camelot.
And at the closing of the day
She loosed the chain, and down she lay;
The broad stream bore her far away,
　　The Lady of Shalott.

Lying, robed in snowy white
That loosely flew to left and right —
The leaves upon her falling light —
Through the noises of the night
　　She floated down to Camelot;
And as the boat-head wound along
The willowy hills and fields among,
They heard her singing her last song,
　　The Lady of Shalott.

Heard a carol, mournful, holy,
Chanted loudly, chanted lowly,
Till her blood was frozen slowly,
And her eyes were darkened wholly,
　　Turned to towered Camelot.
For ere she reached upon the tide
The first house by the water-side,
Singing in her song she died,
　　The Lady of Shalott.

Under tower and balcony,
By garden-wall and gallery,
A gleaming shape she floated by,
Dead-pale between the houses high,
　　Silent into Camelot.
Out upon the wharfs they came,
Knight and burgher, lord and dame,
And round the prow they read her name,
　　The Lady of Shalott.

Who is this? and what is here?
And in the lighted palace near
Died the sound of royal cheer;
And they crossed themselves for fear,
　　All the knights at Camelot;
But Lancelot mused a little space;
He said, 'She has a lovely face;
God in his mercy lend her grace,
　　The Lady of Shalott.'

Alfred Lord Tennyson

ISBN 9780170264907

Reading for meaning

1   You should be able to picture what is happening without knowing the meaning of
    every word, but it is still a good idea to look up any words you do not understand. This
    may include: *wold, shallop, casement, churls, page, ambling pad, bower-eaves, red-cross
    knight, gemmy, blazoned baldric, prow, countenance, burgher, grace.*

    Annotate the meanings around the poem.

2   Now look at the parts of the poem we have highlighted for you. Each is a technique
    and/or important detail. Can you identify the techniques and explain the effect
    or importance of the words? We have completed two for you as a guide to what is
    expected. You will be able to use these notes as you answer the questions that follow.

SETTING (Time, place and social background all have a bearing on this poem).

3   To show that you can see where the events are taking place and what is happening use
    this storyboard to draw a picture showing the scene in Parts I, II, III, IV.

Part I	Part II
Part III	**Part IV**

ISBN 9780170264907

PLOT

A narrative poem tells a story. In your own words briefly explain the plot-line of this poem. Write it in the four parts that the poem is divided into.

Part I _____

_____

_____

Part II _____

_____

_____

Part III _____

_____

_____

Part IV _____

_____

_____

CHARACTER

The Lady is the main character. How does the poet reveal her character? (Ask yourself: does he show what she looks like? What she does? What she says? What she feels? Why she makes her decisions?)

_____

_____

_____

_____

_____

Sir Lancelot is the other named character. How is he described? What is his impact on the Lady? Why does he have this impact? What is his role at the end of the poem?

_____

_____

_____

_____

_____

ISBN 9780170264907

ATMOSPHERE

Think about how the atmosphere changes as the story progresses and how the poet shows these changes. Look particularly at verses 2, 5, 8, 12, 13, 17. Consider colours, rhythm (including length of words), rhyme, sounds, symbols etc.

_____
_____
_____
_____
_____
_____
_____

THEME

What, in your opinion, is the theme of the poem? (You might consider the role of women in Victorian society, the idea of unrequited love, the way an artist or writer can be isolated from the world while painting or writing about life, art vs real experience, romantic tragedy etc.)

_____
_____
_____
_____
_____
_____
_____

Look at this painting which illustrates the poem. Explain what you can see that shows the painter's understanding of the story. In other words, what are the visual-verbal links?

_____
_____
_____
_____
_____

Visual text

Some students enjoy studying visual text more than written text. A visual text may seem more straightforward and simple to understand, but don't be fooled into thinking it is easy!

The word *Visual* might suggest that a visual text is something that is merely seen, but in actual fact it is something that you *read* in the same way as you read a piece of writing.

Visual text are often complex in both their design and their use of language.

HERE IS A *Visual*

What have you 'read'? List what you can tell about this person from this photograph.

_____

_____

_____

_____

ISBN 9780170264907

⚬— So how much do you remember?

Seeing as this section is about visual text, we decided to remind you visually of the knowledge and skills you should be bringing to this text type.

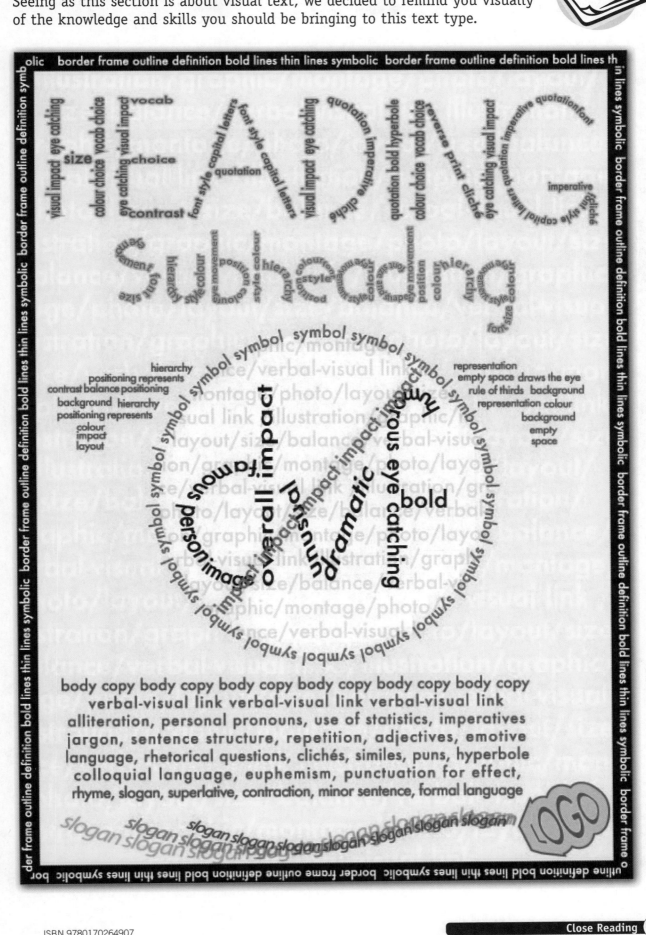

This visual has been annotated for you to draw your attention to some of its features.

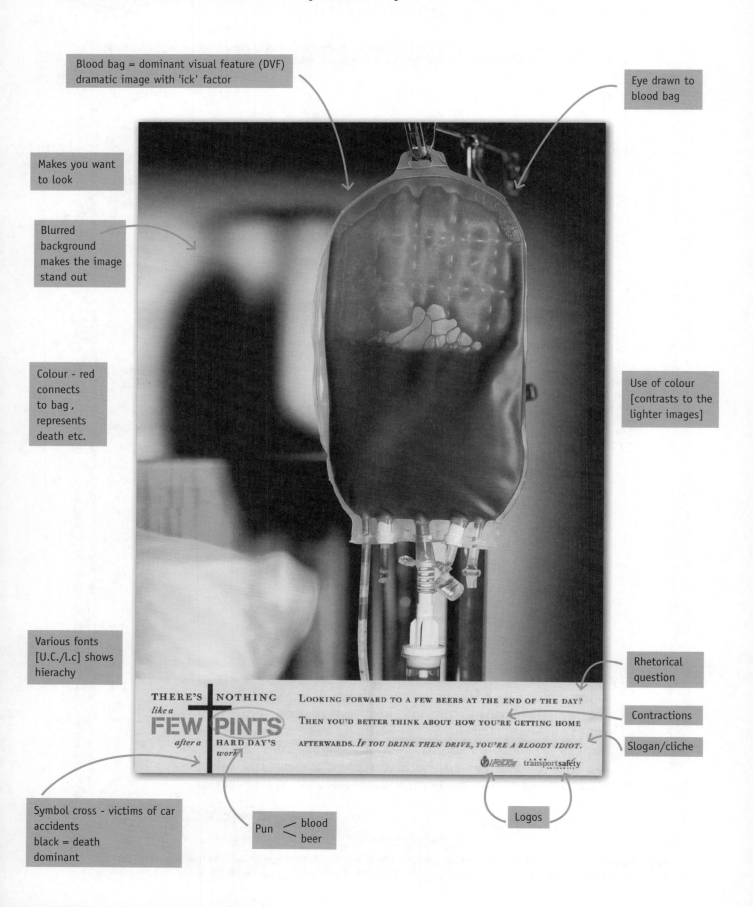

Blood bag = dominant visual feature (DVF) dramatic image with 'ick' factor

Eye drawn to blood bag

Makes you want to look

Blurred background makes the image stand out

Colour - red connects to bag, represents death etc.

Use of colour [contrasts to the lighter images]

Various fonts [U.C./l.c] shows hierachy

Rhetorical question

Contractions

Slogan/cliche

Symbol cross - victims of car accidents black = death dominant

Pun < blood beer

Logos

THERE'S NOTHING *like a* FEW PINTS *after a* HARD DAY'S *work*

LOOKING FORWARD TO A FEW BEERS AT THE END OF THE DAY? THEN YOU'D BETTER THINK ABOUT HOW YOU'RE GETTING HOME AFTERWARDS. *IF YOU DRINK THEN DRIVE, YOU'RE A BLOODY IDIOT.*

ISBN 9780170264907

Before you go further ...

1 Complete the following chart.

What is it **about**?	Who is the **audience**?	What is the **style**?	What is the **purpose**?

Answer the following questions in as much detail as possible.

1 Why does this advertisement attract attention?

_____

_____

_____

2 What is the intended message of the advertisement?

_____

_____

_____

3 Explain the pun used in this advertisement.

_____

_____

_____

4 The designer of this advertisement has used a symbol. Identify the symbol and explain its purpose.

_____

_____

_____

5 Why has the last sentence in the body copy been written in italics?

_____

_____

_____

ISBN 9780170264907

6 This advertisement has been designed for the viewer's eye to move through the poster starting at the dominant visual feature and ending at the logos. Clearly describe how this movement takes place.

_____

_____

_____

_____

_____

_____

_____

_____

_____

_____

New to you might be ... imperative

When something is 'imperative' it must be done. Therefore, in grammar the word means 'command'. Imperatives are used to give orders, commands and instructions. They are very common in advertising, trying to provoke the consumer into action, for example:

- Buy now!
- Eat at Joe's.
- Shop at Sam's Supermarket.
- Make the right choice – choose Charlie's.

Listen to the TV advertising and you will hear many imperatives. Listen to your parents and you will hear plenty, too.

- Get up now.
- Tidy your room.
- Turn off the TV.
- Finish your homework.
- Go to bed.

An aside on ... the verbal-visual link

Let's take a minute to remind ourselves about the importance of the verbal-visual link.
Whenever a visual text is put together there is always a strong focus on the links that exist between the verbal and the visual elements. Sometimes the link will be obvious at a glance but in other cases the body copy will extend the link further.

Spend a few minutes looking carefully at a visual text. Notice the details in the drawing or the photographs. Read the words. Look around the edges at any logos or borders.

You need to LOOK with your brain as well as your eyes!

ISBN 9780170264907

"I finally found my son under **a huge kauri,** captivated by the dawn chorus. I'd already lost my daughter to **a gigantic tarantula."**

Dawn comes around every ten minutes at the Auckland Museum.

Stand beneath the towering kauri that dominates one of our Natural History galleries and listen. An unmistakable burst of birdsong will soon envelop you and if you look down, you'll be able to make out a brown kiwi at the foot of the forest giant.

You'd be forgiven for expecting it to shuffle off through the undergrowth, it looks so lifelike. So too, do the gigantic spiders in the Museum's award-winning Discovery Centre - until they move and you realise that they are indeed alive.

The Centre is a wonderfully hands-on experience and just one of the many surprises in store at the Auckland War Memorial Museum, our richest storehouse of knowledge, rarities and memories.

It's time to bring the whole family along and let them get lost.

Infoline: 09 306 7067

Auckland Museum
Te Papa Whakahiku

Real Treasures. Real Tales.

Care and maintenance of our vast collection is expensive and a $5 donation per adult is requested. Children, of course, are free.

Before you go further …

1 Complete the following chart.

What is it **about**?	Who is the **audience**?	What is the **style**?	What is the **purpose**?

2 Re-read the visual text and, using a highlighter, select and annotate the different features (verbal, visual, layout) you can see.

Answer the following questions in as much detail as possible.

1 Give TWO examples of how balance is created in this static image.

i _____

_____

ii _____

_____

2 Identify THREE verbal-visual links in this static image.

i _____

_____

ii _____

_____

iii _____

_____

3 Identify ONE visual and ONE verbal feature that link to Maori in this static image.

Visual _____

_____

Verbal _____

_____

4 Explain why the chosen colours are used in this static image.

_____

_____

_____

5 The body copy ends with an imperative (command). What is it telling us to do?

_____

_____

_____

ISBN 9780170264907

6 What do the two minor sentences – 'Real Treasures. Real Tales.' – suggest about the museum?

_____

_____

_____

Practice visual 2

Before you go further ...

1 Complete the following chart.

What is it **about**?	Who is the **audience**?	What is the **style**?	What is the **purpose**?

2 Re-read the visual text and, using a highlighter, select and annotate the different features (verbal, visual, layout) you can see.

Answer the following questions in as much detail as possible.

1 'Completely', 'utterly' and 'indisputably' are all examples of?

_____

_____

_____

2 Why have they chosen to compare the amount of blackcurrants grown to rugby fields?

_____

_____

_____

3 How has balance been used in this image?

_____

_____

_____

_____

4 Explain the pun 'put the Kiwi in New Zealand Ribena'.

_____

_____

_____

5 Why does the company want to sell the fact that the blackcurrants are grown in New Zealand, despite Ribena being made elsewhere?

_____

_____

_____

ISBN 9780170264907

6　Describe the tone of this advertisement.

_____

_____

7　Comment on the choice of colours in this advertisement.

_____

_____

_____

8　How has the designer made this advertisement appealing to the reader? Use evidence to support your answer.

_____

_____

_____

_____

_____

_____

_____

9　List all the connections you can find between the verbal and the visual elements of the advertisement.

_____

_____

_____

_____

_____

_____

ISBN 9780170264907

Before you go further ...

1 Complete the following chart.

What is it **about**?	Who is the **audience**?	What is the **style**?	What is the **purpose**?

2 Re-read the visual text and, using a highlighter, select and annotate the different features (verbal, visual, layout) you can see.

Answer the following questions in as much detail as possible.

1 Identify the verbal and visual techniques used in the headline (below) of the text.

Don't get stuck inside for the next 40 years!

get fresh

get a future in the dairy industry

Verbal	Visual

2 The reader is encouraged to read through all of this visual text by the careful positioning of words and pictures. Explain the route that the reader's eye takes through this image, e.g. where you should start, where you move to, and why.

a Start with ... _____

_____

b ... and move to ... _____

_____

c ... and move to ... _____

_____

d ... then ... _____

_____

e ... finally ... _____

_____

3 This visual text has been designed so that its style will appeal to a youthful market. How does it achieve this?

_____

_____

_____

_____

_____

4 Explain the link between the black and white drawings that form part of background of the image and the words used the image. What is the purpose of these verbal-visual links?

_____

_____

_____

_____

_____

_____

_____

_____

_____

_____

New to you might be ... hyperbole

We wanted to take the time to introduce what may be a new term to many of you. Hyperbole is figurative language where an exaggeration is created to aid imagery. It may be used to show emphasis or make a point in an entertaining way, or it can be used to make fun of someone or something.

Hyperbole is used a lot in humorous poems or light-hearted prose. Comedians also use it to make jokes.

For example:
> My sister uses so much makeup that she broke the chisel trying to get it off last night.
> My teacher is so old, they have already nailed the coffin shut.
> I think of you a million times a day.

YOU DO:

Underline the exaggerated statement in the following sentences:
1 My car is so old, it is pulled by a horse.
2 My grandfather is so slow, I miss two shows when he walks in front of the television.
3 My brother is so tall, he has to duck to walk under the telephone lines.
4 My sister has such long legs, she needs to sit in the backseat to drive.
5 His long legs turned to jelly.

ISBN 9780170264907

On your Own

○ Practice makes perfect

By now you will have spent a fair bit of time honing your Close Reading skills. You will need these skills at the end of the year as your ability to close read will be assessed in the external examinations.

The achievement standard requires reading a range of short texts, or extracts, that you have not previously studied, and writing a response to questions that test your understanding of ideas, style and language features.

In our study of English you close read text often. The difference here is that in an external assessment you will not have the luxury of hearing the piece read by your teacher, discussing the text with your teacher and your classmates or writing your responses in consultation with others. In an external assessment you are on your own.

Of course you cannot consult a dictionary in an assessment, now can you read something aloud, but as you *prepare for* this kind of test use all the tools at your disposal. You might try to understand a text without a dictionary but then use one to explain some vocabulary. This will illustrate to you how important it is to extend you own vocabulary.

1. Make sure that you understand the text.
2. Read the text several times.
3. Check meanings of words that you don't fully understand. Annotate (write on the edge of) the text with your meanings.
4. Annotate the text with notes about what you think the text is saying.
5. Highlight effective use of figurative language.
6. Note down what you think the message/theme of the text is.
7. Add any personal opinions you think about as you read the text. Your personal response is always important.
8. Read each question carefully, highlighting the key words to be sure you answer all parts of the question.
9. Think about and make brief notes about your answer before you begin writing.
10. Essentially you are holding you own private discussion about the text before you begin. Time spent thinking and planning an answer is never a waste of time.

BUT TIME IS IMPORTANT:

External assessments will have time constraints. It is likely you will have an hour to look at a minimum of 3 passages. This give you roughly 20 minutes per passage. Hence why we make you practice so much! The work you put into 'learning' to close read now will help you deal with the pressure of doing the same thing in an assessment environment.

Practice 1

Read the poem carefully and answer the questions that follow.

Why Don't You Talk To Me?

Why do I post my love letters in a hollow log?
Why put my lips to a knothole in a tree
And whisper your name?
The spiders spread their nets
And catch the sun,   5
And by my foot in the dry grass
Ants rebuild a broken city.
Butterflies pair in the wind,
And the yellow bee,
His holsters packed with bread,   10
Rides the blue air like a drunken cowboy.
More and more I find myself
Talking to the sea.
I am alone with my footsteps.
I watch the tide recede,   15
And I am left with miles of shining sand.
Why don't you talk to me?

Alistair Campbell

1 Describe the structure of verse 1.

_____

_____

2 Name the creatures that the poet brings to our notice in verse 2. What qualities do the creatures share?

_____

_____

3 Why does the bee remind the poet of a 'drunken cowboy'?

_____

_____

4 Comment on the placement of the last line of the poem and its relevance to the whole poem's meaning.

_____

_____

5 What do you think has happened to make the person in the poem feel this way?

_____

_____

ISBN 9780170264907

Practice 2

Read the passage carefully and answer the questions that follow.

> The sea smelt rotten: the waves churning up the sea floor and spitting its contents onto the grey sand. The clouds hung thick and heavy with bits of light lingering in the west. No one was at the beach, thank goodness.
>
> Simon sat for a while seeing nothing, feeling the weight of sadness clinging to him. If he was a girl he would probably cry now but fear had crept inside and sat waiting, though he had no idea what he was afraid of.
>
> Without his beloved drink, Simon was unable to ignore the pain that pressed firmly into his heart. He knew he was hurting others but didn't have the strength to stop himself. He was a coward.
>
> Just like Proctor, who though he might say the thing with Abigail was over, still burned with lust for her. Simon felt just the same way about alcohol. His blessed fog. The grey mist that embraced him, comforted him. All he had to do was walk down to the tavern and pick up a bottle right now and he'd be back in the familiar place.
>
> Simon pulled out his wallet. It was empty. He sighed. Just as well.
>
> He watched someone swimming strongly toward a boat which rocked out in the bay. The strokes were constant, rhythmic and Simon was full of envy. Right now if he tried to do that he would probably drown. He was more at home in an ocean of alcohol.
>
> He turned away. Is that how it was to be? Was that how it was for him? Was the Simon Hassell that used to be, gone, drowned in a hundred bottles of vodka? The pounding waves drummed the questions as he walked along the sand.
>
> Like hell.
>
> He was not going to let his life eke out of him, like Jesse's blood on the road. Sooner or later he would have to face the demons.
>
> *Compulsion*, Tania Kelly Roxborogh

1 Why was the phrase 'thank goodness' used to end the third sentence?

_____

_____

_____

2 Identify an example of personification and explain what it suggests.

_____

_____

_____

3 In your own words explain why Simon thought he was a coward.

_____

_____

_____

_____

4   Why is Simon pleased he has no money?

_____

_____

_____

5   Comment on the connection between the first four lines and the rest of the passage.

_____

_____

_____

_____

_____

An aside on ... tone

If you look up the word 'tone' in a dictionary - and this would be a good idea - you will see that it has many meanings. Some meanings are to do with music, some are to do with sounds, some are to do with colour. In close reading you are using this meaning:

> 'A particular style in discourse or writing, which expresses the person's sentiment or reveals his character; also *spec.* in literary criticism, an author's attitude to his subject matter or audience; the distinctive mood created by this.' (OED)

When you are looking into the tone of a passage or text:

- Consider the vocabulary the writer chooses. Words can have a literal and figurative meanings. All the ones chosen will have been chosen for a purpose.

- Think about the way words and syllables have distinct sounds: hard, soft etc. You will be aware of this when you read poetry. It applies to prose, too.

- Look at the way the words are put together. Long sentences? Short sentences? Does this create any special effects? Is anything missing in the description?

- Are you affected by the words? Do you feel sad? Or happy? Or alarmed? Or surprised? Or persuaded? Or amused? Or...?

These questions should help you to identify the tone of the passage more easily.

ISBN 9780170264907

Practice 3

Read the passage carefully and answer the questions that follow.

Mana Wahine

Now that the Manu Ariki competition is over, the girls have calmed down. But it was an experience never to be forgotten. As soon as I walked through the gates to the powhiri, it was like something entered me, but I didn't know what it was. I was still myself, though. Seeing the groups doing their first waiata, showing off their talents to everyone ... but that was just the powhiri. We still had the whole two days to go yet.

Finally it was time to get the competition on the way. It was ace seeing the groups battling it out on stage, pushing themselves to a higher and higher standard. But the best part for me was when the other groups would stand and tautoko the performing groups. It was like warriors challenging. Dust rising from the ground from the stamping of the takahia, voices carried above and past the hills, eyes lighting up like light bulbs in the dark, and the actions, each with its own meaning.

It was really something. You could see the tears filling the eyes of the crowd. When Turakina stood to perform, we were the centre of attention. Even though I was the guitarist, the crowd could still see every movement I made, so I was very careful.

The waiata we did, especially the haka and our entry, filled the crowd with excitement – and the groups we were competing against with envy. Even on stage as a performer I could see the crowd's eyes light up when they saw Te Kotiro Tuturu in their red, black and white.

We performed like the sea: one moment beautiful and flowing, the next, stamping our feet, working the patu, pulling our lips down, and showing the whites of our eyes. And being inside the shell with our waha nui, the sound effects were like a bomb!

After our performance we were commented on like we were superstars or something. It was massive. Prize-giving came. Groups were in bunches in front of the stage, anxiously waiting for their names to be called out as first prize winners. We didn't win, but came second, and that was massive. It was awesome, too, everyone cheering and clapping, the drumbeats of the Pacific Islanders, and once again the waiata of the groups.

It was finally over: people saying their congratulations, their final goodbyes, hugs and kisses, and I can't forget the tears of the girls. They spread around the two winning roopu, Tuhoe Potiki and Turakina. When we finally got to our bus, girls were still clinging on to their cuzzies and bros making it harder to say goodbye, but finally we unclenched them and headed back to school. On the way back, the girls were singing and doing the haka, never to forget the experience of Manu Ariki.

Terri Hudson, Turakina Maori Girls' College

1   In your own words explain what you understand about the competition.

_____

_____

2   What is the role of the narrator in her group's performance and what is her attitude to her role?

_____

_____

3 In your own words, explain what narrator means when she says 'We performed like the sea' (paragraph 5).

_____

_____

4 The writer uses several other similes in the passage. Choose TWO and explain the effect of each one.

Simile one:

_____

_____

Explanation:

_____

_____

_____

Simile two:

_____

_____

Explanation:

_____

_____

_____

5 How does the language used show the age of the narrator? Give at least THREE examples.

_____

_____

_____

_____

_____

_____

_____

_____

_____

_____

ISBN 9780170264907

Practice 4

Read the poem carefully and answer the questions that follow.

Thistles

Against the rubber tongues of cows and the hoeing
Hands of men
Thistles spike the summer air
Or crackle open under a blue-black pressure.

Every one a revengeful burst
Of resurrection, a grasped fistful
Of splintered weapons and Icelandic frost thrust up

From the underground stain of a decayed Viking.*
They are like pale hair and the gutturals of dialects.
Every one manages a plume of blood

Then they grow grey, like men.
Mown down, it is a feud. Their sons appear,
Stiff with weapons, fighting back over the same ground.

Ted Hughes

*Viking: a member of the Scandinavian people who raided and invaded
various parts of northwest Europe from the 8th to the 11th century AD.

Anyone who has fought a battle with thistles in a paddock or garden will understand this poem's meaning.

1 This poem reveals the thistle as a violent presence. How does the poet link the plant to violence? Focus on lines 4-7 and 11-12.

_____

_____

_____

2 The poem creates several images. Explain each one listed here and say how effective it is.

a the rubber tongues of cows

_____

_____

_____

b spike the summer air

_____

_____

_____

c crackle open

_____

_____

_____

d a plume of blood

_____

_____

_____

e grow grey, like men

_____

_____

_____

3 Relate this poem to New Zealand.

_____

_____

_____

_____

_____

_____

An aside on ... succeeding at Unfamiliar Text

Just to recap, if you wish to achieve this Achievement Standard then you must:

ANSWER THE QUESTION. Read the whole question. Note the key words in the question.
Note that 'Identify' and 'Explain' are different instructions: one generally follows the other.

ANSWER ALL THE QUESTIONS. The questions build up a whole picture of your understanding.
Don't pick and choose.

WRITE YOUR ANSWER CLEARLY. Take a moment to think it out, even jot down notes, before you
write any words at all.

SUPPORT YOUR ANSWER. Quote examples from the text. Don't make up your own examples.
Paraphrase (restate more simply, or in fewer words) if need be.

THINK ABOUT THE WHOLE TEXT. What is this text? Who is it for? What else have you read similar
to it?

The more you read; the more widely you read, the better you will cope with this Achievement
Standard. See our reading list on page 160 of this book.

ISBN 9780170264907

Just one more thing ...

Achievement English @ Year 11 teaches you strategies to help you close read unfamiliar text. We have used a variety of types of both texts and questions to help you develop your own close reading skills. We have asked you to practise identifying key style features and explain how and why the author chose to use them. We have also focused on making you familiar with language terms, and their definitions, so you will be able to use them with authority as you explain what you understand about the texts.

Now that you are familiar with the more direct question there is another type of question that we would like to introduce to you. It is commonly referred to as a 'Scaffolded' Question. What is a 'scaffold'? A scaffold is a support structure, usually around a building being developed. However, when talking about a scaffolded question in English it refers to a question that offers you support, or hints, as to how to answer the question. Such a question will demand a longer, more detailed and self-structured answer.

Scaffolded questions will not ask about an isolated technique or meaning or purpose. Instead, they will ask a wider question but will give you ideas about how to answer them in depth and detail. Always use the clues.

So what does this mean?

- Instead of being given several short, specific questions you are given one or two more general questions.
- These questions demand a longer, more structured answer.
- You are often given 'hints' about what sort of information you might include in your answer.

Is that important?

- Your answer will be assessed as N, A, M, or E depending on the detail in the response you provide.
- Show that you have heeded the advice you have been given by planning your answer carefully around the hints.
- Your aim is a response that clearly expresses your understanding of the text.

Here is an example of the kind of question we are talking about:

Look at Text B as a whole.

Explain how the poet's feelings about the friendship are developed. Support your answer with examples from the text. In your answer, you could cover some of the following aspects:

- ideas
- imagery
- style
- structure
- narrative point-of-view.

Here the question gives you the overall topic of your answer and five potential points you might mention if you can find examples in the text. (If you cannot, do not use the point!)

Here is a second example:

Explain how the writer shows **what the experience of the fire is like for Federico**. Support your answer with examples from the text.

You could use one or more of the following ideas as a starting point for your answer:

* the techniques, including language features, that the writer uses to show Federico's experience
* the importance of the title
* the contrast between Sylvia and Federico.

Here the question specifically invites you to use one or more of these bullet point ideas in your answer. Always try to explain the effect of any language technique you identify.

How do you tackle this kind of question? Like any other question you are asked!

You are used to answering very specific short questions relating to text. *Why is the word 'xxx' used? What does this metaphor suggest?* etc These answers are very similar, they are usually just asking you to think about the text as a whole.

As with any other question, the key thing is that you actually **answer the question**. Don't worry about the string of empty lines below the question that you feel have to fill with writing.

Use this strategy to help you:

- Read the question twice.
- Underline key words.
- Read and re-read the passage.
- Underline or highlight detail that looks important to you as you go.
- Go back to the hints or bullet points.
- Check if there's anything else in the passage you want to highlight.
- Take a few minutes to plan your answer. Think of it as a small essay.
- Make sure you are using specific language terms if possible.
- Check that you always support any point you make with an example.
- Write your answer.
- Re-read your answer – **have you answered the question?**

ISBN 9780170264907

Building an answer

A detailed answer needs just that – detail. Some students find this easier to understand in terms of points made. Here is the first verse of a poem **Little City** by *Robert Horan* about a spider.

> Spider, from his flaming sleep,
> staggers out into the window frame;
> swings out from the red den where he slept
> to nest in the gnarled glass.
> Fat hero, burnished cannibal
> lets down a frail ladder and ties a knot,
> sways down to a landing with furry grace.

Now a question about this verse might ask what does the poet wish to draw the reader's attention to in this first verse.

A very simple answer might be

> *He wants the reader to notice how the spider moves.*

Support for this answer might be:

> *He uses verbs 'staggers, swings, sways' to describe these movements.*

A slightly more detailed answer might also say:

> *The poet also describes the spider as fat but attractively shiny and graceful in his movements.*

Here's a tip – to write a detailed insightful response make sure you think about what all the important words mean – both denotation and connotation.

A more carefully constructed and detailed answer might say:

> *The poet wants the reader to visualise the spider emerging from a dark place, "red den" moving unsteadily at first, he 'staggers' and then more confidently, he 'swings' to a deliberate position. He will 'nest' deliberately, purposefully, set up a home for himself, against the window.*

> *In the second part of the verse the spider is described as a "fat hero" an oxymoron, heroes are not usually fat so there is immediately some suggestion that he is not a conventional hero while suggesting he is brave and at the centre of this adventure. The spider is the described as a 'burnished cannibal' glossy, shiny but deadly to his own kind. This introduces what the spider does next: he begins to construct his web.*

> *The writer stresses the delicacy of the spider web, using the oxymoron" a frail ladder", and describes the skilfulness of the spider as he now 'sways' and lands with 'grace'.*

And a comment of more depth might also add:

> *There is discord in this first verse between the attractive appearance and admiration of the spider's movement and the expected inevitable outcome for other insects ,of his appearance and industry.*

You might like to go over these answers and highlight the number of points the student has made. We calculate 2, 3 and 8. If you plan your answer first you can list your points and check that you've made them all at the end.

ISBN 9780170264907

Let's look at a question together

Let's look closely at a short poem written by Christina Rossetti. Read the poem carefully.

Hurt No Living Thing

Hurt no living thing;
Ladybird nor butterfly,
Nor moth with dusty wing,
Nor cricket chirping cheerily,
Nor grasshopper so light of leap,
Nor dancing gnat, nor beetle fat,
Nor harmless worms that creep.

Christina Rossetti

First ...

Find, highlight and annotate as many examples of the following as you can:

- punctuation
- nouns
- rhyme
- repetition
- alliteration
- imperative.

ISBN 9780170264907

Using your annotations above, answer the following question in as much detail as possible.

1 What is the poem's message? How is that message conveyed?

In your answer you might mention structure, vocabulary, repetition

(Use the hints to help you scaffold your response, but you can mention other techniques if you wish).

_____

_____

_____

_____

_____

_____

_____

_____

_____

_____

_____

_____

_____

_____

_____

_____

_____

_____

_____

_____

_____

_____

_____

_____

_____

ISBN 9780170264907

On your own

Now it is time for you to have a go on your own. Below is a passage from *Adventures of Huckleberry Finn* by Mark Twain. Read the passage at least twice, annotating important features.

You don't know about me, without you have read a book by the name of "The Adventures of Tom Sawyer," but that ain't no matter. That book was made by Mr. Mark Twain, and he told the truth, mainly. There was things which he stretched, but mainly he told the truth. That is nothing.

I never seen anybody but lied, one time or another, without it was Aunt Polly¬— Tom's Aunt Polly she is—and Mary, and the Widow Douglas, is all told about in that book—which is mostly a true book; with some stretchers, as I said before.

Now the way that the book winds up, is this: Tom and me found the money that the robbers hid in the cave, and it made us rich. We got six thousand dollars apiece—all gold. It was an awful sight of money when it was piled up. Well, Judge Thatcher, he took it and put it out at interest, and it fetched us a dollar a day apiece, all the year round—more than a body could tell what to do with. The Widow Douglas, she took me for her son, and allowed she would sivilize me; but it was rough living in the house all the time, considering how dismal regular and decent the widow was in all her ways; and so when I couldn't stand it no longer I lit out. I got into my old rags, and my sugar-hogshead* again, and was free and satisfied. But Tom Sawyer, he hunted me up and said he was going to start a band of robbers and I might join if I would go back to the widow and be respectable. So I went back.

The widow she cried over me, and called me a poor lost lamb, and she called me a lot of other names, too, but she never meant no harm by it. She put me in them new clothes again, and I couldn't do nothing but sweat and sweat, and feel all cramped up. Well, then, the old thing commenced again. The widow rung a bell for supper, and you had to come to time. When you got to the table you couldn't go right to eating, but you had to wait for the widow to tuck down her head and grumble a little over the victuals, though there warn't really anything the matter with them. That is, nothing only everything was cooked by itself. In a barrel of odds and ends it is different; things get mixed up, and the juice kind of swaps around, and things go better.

After supper she got out her book and learned me abut Moses and the Bulrushers; and I was in a sweat to find out all about him; but by-and-by she let it out that Moses had been dead a considerable long time; so then I didn't care no more about him; because I don't take no stock of dead people.

Pretty soon I wanted to smoke, and asked the widow to let me. But she wouldn't. She said it was a mean practice and wasn't clean, and I must try not to do it any more. That is just the way with some people. They get down on a thing when they don't know nothing about it. Here she was bothering about Moses, which was no kin to her, and no use to anybody being gone, you see, yet finding a power of fault with me for doing a thing that had some good in it. And she took snuff too; of course that was all right, because she done it herself.

*sugar-hogshead – large barrel to hold sugar

ISBN 9780170264907

1 What is the narrative voice of this novel? What do you learn about this character in the opening paragraph?

_____

_____

_____

_____

_____

_____

_____

_____

_____

_____

_____

_____

_____

_____

2 What details does Paragraph 2 add to your knowledge about the narrator?

_____

_____

_____

_____

_____

_____

_____

_____

_____

_____

_____

_____

_____

_____

_____

ISBN 9780170264907

3 Looking at the passage as a whole, how does the author continue to develop your understanding of the narrator? Do not repeat anything you have already said, but you might mention:

- grammar
- sentence structure
- thoughts

- dialect words
- pronunciation
- opinions

- phrasing
- actions
- actions

_____

_____

_____

_____

_____

_____

_____

_____

_____

_____

_____

_____

_____

_____

_____

_____

_____

_____

_____

_____

_____

4 **Extension.** How is the author commenting on society through this passage?

_____

_____

_____

_____

_____

_____

_____

_____

ISBN 9780170264907

Language Lists

Although we have divided these techniques into lists linking them to specific text, they may well be relevant to more than one type of text. For example, you might find a rhetorical question in a speech, a formal essay, a poem or a magazine article.

LANGUAGE TECHNIQUES FOR WRITTEN TEXT

NOUN
Naming word.
E.g. plum, Peter, power, pod

COMMON NOUN
Name of ordinary, everyday objects. Can be preceded by 'a/an' or 'the'.
E.g. a pear, an apple, the banana

PROPER NOUN
Name of person, place etc. Always begins with a capital letter.
E.g. Alan to Zebedee, Africa to Zanzibar

ABSTRACT NOUN
Name of something that we cannot see, touch or measure. You can give it ...but you can't wrap it up.
E.g. air, authority, amazement

COLLECTIVE NOUN
Name of a group of objects, people or creatures. A *collection* of similar things or people – that is why it's called a *collective* noun.
E.g. band, orchestra, ensemble, quartet, group

PRONOUN
A pronoun is used in the place of a noun. Avoids always repeating a name.
E.g. I, me, mine, you, yours

ADJECTIVE
An adjective describes a noun. Adds detail to names and nouns.
E.g. black, bold, big, brave, bronzed

COMPARATIVE ADJECTIVE
A form of adjective that compares things. Shows the difference between two things.
E.g. blacker, bolder, bigger, braver, more bronzed

SUPERLATIVE ADJECTIVE
A form of adjective that describes the best or the most from three or more things. It's also pointing out difference.
E.g. blackest, boldest, biggest, bravest, most bronzed

VERB
A word that expresses doing or being. Somebody or something does something. Something or somebody is something.
E.g. I eat, I drink, I am (happy), I was (thirsty)

ADVERB
Gives you more information about a verb. Adverbs tell you when, where or how something is done.
E.g. cheerfully, thirstily, happily, miserably

CONJUNCTION
A conjunction links two or more sentences into a single sentence. Known as a 'joining word'. Conjunctions are usually found in the middle of sentences, but not always. Conjunctions can also join words, phrases or clauses.
E.g. and, so, but, yet, or, after, because

PREPOSITION
A preposition tells us the position or place of something in relation to something else. Prepositions are usually 'small words'.
E.g. at, by, for, on, in, of, under

EUPHEMISM
A euphemism expresses an unpleasant or uncomfortable or embarrassing situation in a more sensitive, kind and tactful manner. The purpose is to soften the blow, protect feelings or to be politically correct.
E.g. My grandfather passed away.

PUN
A pun is a clever play on words which are similar in sound but different meaning. The double meaning is used to convey humour. Puns are often used in headlines, advertising, jokes and riddles.
E.g. P&O holidays: living the cruisy lifestyle.

CLICHÉ
Trite and worn out phrases that communicate an image easily, and don't need too much thinking about.
E.g. I could eat a horse.

COLLOQUIAL LANGUAGE
The word colloquial is used to define language that is used in casual conversation. It is likely to be even more ungrammatical, fractured and full of cliché than informal language. You will use colloquial expressions in your everyday conversations with friends and family.
E.g. G'day. You coming out? I'm off now.

SLANG
Slang is very informal language that is usually vivid, playful and short-lived. Each generation formulates its own slang and these words are usually 'passing phases'. We would have given you an example but it would be out-of-date before the book was printed!

JARGON
Jargon is used by a particular group, profession or culture. Often, other people do not understand the words and so it can seem like pretentious or meaningless language. Jargon may be highly technical.
E.g. My new bike is awesome. It has a Cro-mo frame and alloy rims and the groupset are all high spec'd.

See also: Language Techniques for Poetic Text

LANGUAGE TECHNIQUES FOR POETIC TEXT

IMAGERY
The creation of images or pictures to help writers achieve their intended purpose. An image can be created using different devices such as similes, assonance or adjectives.

SIMILE
A simile is a direct comparison that always contains the word 'as' or 'like'.
E.g. My brother John eats like a pig.
This suggests that John has unpleasant table manners. A simile adds vivid, descriptive details.

METAPHOR
A metaphor is a comparison which does not use like or as. It says that one thing is another.
E.g. My brother John is a pig
This metaphor suggests that John has unpleasant manners, not that he actually is a pig. Metaphors are used to highlight certain qualities of whatever is being described.

EXTENDED METAPHOR
This is a metaphor that is extended over a passage or throughout a poem.

PERSONIFICATION
Personification is where a non-living object is given living qualities, writing of it as if it were a living person. Appearances, actions, thoughts and feelings can all be given human attributes. Personification gives life and energy to images and ideas.
E.g. The vine is strangling that tree.
This gives the idea of the vine as an aggressor with intent to harm and the tree as the victim.

ALLITERATION
Alliteration is the repetition on consonant sounds at the beginning of words placed closely together to create a sound echo.
E.g. A black-backed gull bent like an iron bar slowly
This line has to be read slowly in order to pronounce the words. Therefore it emphasises the strength of the wind against which the bird is flying.
Alliteration is used to:
- add humour or power
- create a mood or feeling
- help the flow or movement of language. Some alliteration is hard ... b and d, while others are soft, calming ... l, s, f
- emphasise important points.

ONOMATOPOEIA
Onomatopoeia uses words that imitate and reproduce real-life sounds and actions.
E.g. The buzz of a chainsaw.
Onomatopoeia helps to increase reality in the text through adding another dimension by suggesting sound as well as meaning.

ASSONANCE
Assonance is the repetition of vowel sounds. The trick is not to think of it as the same letter, but the same sound.
E.g. He climbed high, singing wildly
Clinging to the rock face
Alive, at last.
As with alliteration, assonance allows the poem to flow more quickly or it can slow the poem down as each word is emphasised to reflect the meaning of that part of the poem.

RHYME

Rhyme is the repetition of final vowel and consonant sounds in words.

E.g. She left the web, she left the loom,
She made three paces thro' the room,
She saw the water-lily bloom,
(from The Lady of Shallot, Alfred Lord Tennyson)

Words that sound the same, or almost the same, are likely to make us notice them. Rhyming words can fall anywhere, in the middle of lines, in regular or irregular patterns, but we are most used to them at the end of lines of poetry.

Rhyme is designed to:
* add pleasing sound effects
* provide a disciplined structure
* highlight particular words/phrases
* follow an established pattern.

RHYTHM

The rhythm is the flow and beat of the poem.

E.g. This is the night mail crossing the border
Bringing the cheque and the postal order
(from The Night Mail, W.H Auden)

Here the beat/sound of the train is imitated.

REPETITION

When words or phrases are repeated for emphasis of some kind.

E.g. Veni, vidi, vici. I came, I saw, I conquered.
(Julius Caesar)

Repetition is often used for emphasis and in this case Caesar is pointing out his own importance.

LANGUAGE TECHNIQUES FOR VISUAL TEXT

CONTRAST

Use of two colours for eye-catching contrasts. Designers think about which colours combine effectively. For instance yellow & black, red & black, orange & purple.
E.g. Football team uniforms.

DVF

The Dominant Visual Feature is the central focus of the static image. The point of impact. It may be dominant because of its position, often at the centre of the image.

GRAPHIC/ILLUSTRATION

Graphics are the pictures, photographs, drawings, graphs – everything that is not the writing in an image.

WELL-KNOWN/POPULAR FACES

Many advertisements use someone who is famous to sell a product/service. It may be purely to attract attention *(for example Daniel Carter selling underwear)* or it may be endorsing a product that the celebrity would know about *(for example Lydia Ko advertising golf clubs)*.

FONT (STYLE AND SIZE)

Designers choose the fonts of the text to go with their images carefully. The text must be clear to read (not too elaborate) and in some situations, able to be read from a distance. The font will also aim to reflect the ideas within the image.
E.g. In advertising a children's product the font will be large and colourful while a funeral home is likely to choose an elegant, simple font.

COLOUR

Colours help represent a product or an idea.
E.g. An image designed to sell a cleaning product is likely to have a lot of white to suggest cleanliness

BOLD LINES

Bold shapes and lines help to draw in the eye. Some things are outlined in black to give them definition or to frame certain parts of the whole image.

BACKGROUND

The background may be left plain in order to focus the viewer's attention onto the other features or it may incorporate colour to support its message.
E.g. A green background on an advertisement for a healthy product is not uncommon, for example, as green suggests natural.

UNUSUAL IMAGES

Unusual pictures or layout to make people stop and study the image more closely may be used.

SYMBOLS/LOGOS

Symbolism is where a concrete object is used to represent one or more abstract ideas. It can be words, a shape, a graphic.
E.g. The dove (a material object) represents peace (something abstract).

LAYOUT

Layout is the process of organising forms, shapes, colours and any words into a balanced design. These choices are made with the purpose, topic and audience in mind.

THE VERBAL/VISUAL LINK

Whenever a visual text is put together there is always a strong focus on the links that exist between the verbal and the visual elements.

BALANCE

Designers achieve balance by looking at a layout design as an arrangement of shapes. The easiest way to create balance in a visual text is to treat all the elements as geometric shapes.

RULE OF THIRDS

The rule states that an image can be divided into nine equal parts by two equally-spaced horizontal lines and two equally spaced vertical lines. The four points formed by the intersections of these lines can be used to align features in a visual image.

EMPTY SPACE

Empty space refers to areas of the text that have no text or graphics in them. These areas may not necessarily be printed in the colour 'white', but it is important the colour is the same throughout so that the effect works in the same way.
Empty space is used to:
* prevent the layout looking crowded
* help balance the overall design
* create impact or focus on a certain feature
* help the audience to read the text and graphics in the correct order.

HIERARCHY

The hierarchy of a layout design means the order of importance of different elements and the order in which elements should be viewed or read. When each element is given a grade of importance and designers style or size them as such, it makes it easy for readers to know where to look or read first and where to move their eyes across and into the visual.

HEADLINE

The headline is the main 'title' of the advertisement/image. This will be in the biggest font size. The words are designed to attract attention and provoke the audience to look further.

LEVEL OF LANGUAGE (FORMAL, INFORMAL, COLLOQUIAL, SLANG, JARGON)

The type of language chosen for an advertisement gives us clues about the intended audience.
* If it is feminine and flowery it is most likely aimed at girls or women.
* If it is formal it is most likely advertising something of a serious nature.
* If there is a lot of technical language it would have a very specific audience in mind.
* A lot of slang terms might indicate it is aimed at a youthful audience.

REPETITION

Repetition aids memory. Repeating the product name, slogan and/or key features will help people remember the brand.

RHETORICAL QUESTION

A rhetorical question is a question where the answer is implied. It adds to the persuasive power of the speaker. Often a speaker adds emphasis to a point by putting it in the form of a question, the answer to which supports his or her argument.

Rhetorical questions are designed to get the audience to momentarily stop and think about what is being said.
E.g. What is this one indispensable thing? Need I tell you? It is this – the cellphone.

PUN

A pun is a clever play on words, using two words that are alike in sound but different in meaning. The double meaning is used to convey humour. Headlines make use of puns in order to grab attention.
E.g. Trust British Paints ... Sure Can.
New Indian Restaurant Curries Favour

USE OF ADJECTIVES

Advertisers will often choose words that help us picture the look, taste or texture of the product. Think about what advertisers say about breakfast cereals: *crunchy, wholesome, nutty, tasty.*
Comparative adjectives and superlatives are often used.

SLOGAN

Most companies and services have a slogan (a short, snappy sentence) that is easy to remember.

BODY COPY

Body copy is usually found in a paragraph towards the bottom of an image. These detailed words in a static image are often referred to as the 'small print'.

RHETORICAL QUESTION

A rhetorical question expects no answer because it assumes one. It is used to allow the audience to focus on and consider the posed question.
E.g. Sick of spending hours scrubbing your shower and it still not being clean?
The assumed answer to this question is 'Of course, I am.'

PERSONAL PRONOUNS

Personal pronouns are used to make the audience feel that the advertisement is speaking directly to them. They give a chatty, conversational tone to the piece to make the audience feel included.

ALLITERATION

Alliteration is easy to remember. The audience will be able to recall the catch phrase at another time. Alliteration also makes words flow together more easily and it can highlight key words and ideas.
E.g. Just Juice, NZ Natural

ISBN 9780170264907